Glenview, Illinois • Boston, Massachusetts • Chandler, Arizona • Upper Saddle River, New Jersey

Scott Foresman
Science

The Diamond Edition

Series Authors

Dr. Timothy Cooney
Professor of Earth Science and Science Education
University of Northern Iowa (UNI)
Cedar Falls, Iowa

Dr. Jim Cummins
Professor
Department of Curriculum, Teaching, and Learning
University of Toronto
Toronto, Canada

Dr. James Flood
Distinguished Professor of Literacy and Language
School of Teacher Education
San Diego State University
San Diego, California

Barbara Kay Foots, M.Ed.
Science Education Consultant
Houston, Texas

Dr. M. Jenice Goldston
Associate Professor of Science Education
Department of Elementary Education Programs
University of Alabama
Tuscaloosa, Alabama

Dr. Shirley Gholston Key
Associate Professor of Science Education
Instruction and Curriculum Leadership Department
College of Education
University of Memphis
Memphis, Tennessee

Dr. Diane Lapp
Distinguished Professor of Reading and Language Arts in Teacher Education
San Diego State University
San Diego, California

Sheryl A. Mercier
Classroom Teacher
Dunlap Elementary School
Dunlap, California

Karen L. Ostlund, Ph.D.
UTeach Specialist
College of Natural Sciences
The University of Texas at Austin
Austin, Texas

Dr. Nancy Romance
Professor of Science Education & Principal Investigator
NSF/IERI Science IDEAS Project
Charles E. Schmidt College of Science
Florida Atlantic University
Boca Raton, Florida

Dr. William Tate
Chair and Professor of Education and Applied Statistics
Department of Education
Washington University
St. Louis, Missouri

Dr. Kathryn C. Thornton
Former NASA Astronaut Professor
School of Engineering and Applied Science
University of Virginia
Charlottesville, Virginia

Dr. Leon Ukens
Professor Emeritus
Department of Physics, Astronomy, and Geosciences
Towson University
Towson, Maryland

Steve Weinberg
Consultant
Connecticut Center for Advanced Technology
East Hartford, Connecticut

Photographs
Every effort has been made to secure permission and provide appropriate credit for photographic material. The publisher deeply regrets any omission and pledges to correct errors called to its attention in subsequent editions. Unless otherwise acknowledged, all photographs are the property of Scott Foresman, a division of Pearson Education. Photo locators denoted as follows: Top (T), Center (C), Bottom (B), Left (L), Right (R), Background (Bkgd)

Acknowledgments appear on pages EM 61–63, which constitute an extension of this copyright page.

ISBN-13: 978-0-328-45580-5
ISBN-10:   0-328-45580-6
9   17

Consulting Author

Dr. Michael P. Klentschy
Superintendent
El Centro Elementary School District
El Centro, California

Science Content Consultants

Dr. Frederick W. Taylor
Senior Research Scientist
Institute for Geophysics
Jackson School of Geosciences
The University of Texas at Austin
Austin, Texas

Dr. Ruth E. Buskirk
Senior Lecturer
School of Biological Sciences
The University of Texas at Austin
Austin, Texas

Dr. Cliff Frohlich
Senior Research Scientist
Institute for Geophysics
Jackson School of Geosciences
The University of Texas at Austin
Austin, Texas

Brad Armosky
McDonald Observatory
The University of Texas at Austin
Austin, Texas

Content Consultants

Adena Williams Loston, Ph.D.
Chief Education Officer
Office of the Chief Education Officer

Clifford W. Houston, Ph.D.
Deputy Chief Education Officer for Education Programs
Office of the Chief Education Officer

Frank C. Owens
Senior Policy Advisor
Office of the Chief Education Officer

Deborah Brown Biggs
Manager, Education Flight Projects Office
Space Operations Mission Directorate, Education Lead

Erika G. Vick
NASA Liaison to Pearson Scott Foresman
Education Flight Projects Office

William E. Anderson
Partnership Manager for Education
Aeronautics Research Mission Directorate

Anita Krishnamurthi
Program Planning Specialist
Space Science Education and Outreach Program

Bonnie J. McClain
Chief of Education
Exploration Systems Mission Directorate

Diane Schweizer
Program Scientist
Earth Science Education

Deborah Rivera
Strategic Alliances Manager
Office of Public Affairs
NASA Headquarters

Douglas D. Peterson
Public Affairs Officer, Astronaut Office
Office of Public Affairs
NASA Johnson Space Center

Nicole Cloutier
Public Affairs Officer, Astronaut Office
Office of Public Affairs
NASA Johnson Space Center

Dr. Jennifer J. Wiseman
Hubble Space Scientist Program Scientist
NASA Headquarters

Reviewers

Dr. Maria Aida Alanis
Administrator
Austin ISD
Austin Texas

Melissa Barba
Teacher
Wesley Mathews Elementary
Miami, Florida

Dr. Marcelline Barron
Supervisor/K-12 Math
and Science
Fairfield Public Schools
Fairfield, Connecticut

Jane Bates
Teacher
Hickory Flat Elementary
Canton, Georgia

Denise Bizjack
Teacher Dr. N. H. Jones
Elementary
Ocala, Florida

Latanya D. Bragg
Teacher
Davis Magnet School
Jackson, Mississippi

Richard Burton
Teacher
George Buck Elementary
School 94
Indianapolis, Indiana

Dawn Cabrera
Teacher E.W.F. Stirrup School
Miami, Florida

Barbara Calabro
Teacher
Compass Rose Foundation
Ft. Myers, Florida

Lucille Calvin
Teacher
Weddington Math &
Science School
Greenville, Mississippi

Patricia Carmichael
Teacher
Teasley Middle School
Canton, Georgia

Martha Cohn
Teacher
An Wang Middle School
Lowell, Massachusetts

Stu Danzinger
Supervisor
Community Consolidated
School District 59
Arlington Heights, Illinois

Esther Draper
Supervisor/Science Specialist
Belair Math Science
Magnet School
Pine Bluff, Arkansas

Sue Esser
Teacher
Loretto Elementary
Jacksonville, Florida

Dr. Richard Fairman
Teacher
Antioch University
Yellow Springs, Ohio

Joan Goldfarb
Teacher
Indialantic Elementary
Indialantic, Florida

Deborah Gomes
Teacher
A J Gomes Elementary
New Bedford, Massachusetts

Sandy Hobart
Teacher
Mims Elementary
Mims, Florida

Tom Hocker
Teacher/Science Coach
Boston Latin Academy
Dorchester, Massachusetts

Shelley Jaques
Science Supervisor
Moore Public Schools
Moore, Oklahoma

Marguerite W. Jones
Teacher
Spearman Elementary
Piedmont, South Carolina

Kelly Kenney
Teacher
Kansas City Missouri
School District
Kansas City, Missouri

Carol Kilbane
Teacher
Riverside Elementary School
Wichita, Kansas

Robert Kolenda
Teacher
Neshaminy School District
Langhorne, Pennsylvania

Karen Lynn Kruse
Teacher
St. Paul the Apostle
Yonkers, New York

Elizabeth Loures
Teacher
Point Fermin
Elementary School
San Pedro, California

Susan MacDougall
Teacher
Brick Community Primary
Learning Center
Brick, New Jersey

Jack Marine
Teacher
Raising Horizons Quest
Charter School
Philadelphia, Pennsylvania

Nicola Micozzi Jr.
Science Coordinator
Plymouth Public Schools
Plymouth, Massachusetts

Paula Monteiro
Teacher
A J Gomes Elementary
New Bedford, Massachusetts

Tracy Newallis
Teacher
Taper Avenue Elementary
San Pedro, California

Dr. Eugene Nicolo
Supervisor, Science K-12
Moorestown School District
Moorestown, New Jersey

Jeffry Pastrak
School District of Philadelphia
Philadelphia, Pennsylvania

Helen Pedigo
Teacher
Mt. Carmel Elementary
Huntsville Alabama

Becky Peltonen
Teacher
Patterson Elementary School
Panama City, Florida

Sherri Pensler
Teacher/ESOL
Claude Pepper Elementary
Miami, Florida

Virginia Rogliano
Teacher
Bridgeview Elementary
South Charleston, West
Virginia

Debbie Sanders
Teacher
Thunderbolt Elementary
Orange Park, Florida

Grethel Santamarina
Teacher
E.W.F. Stirrup School
Miami, Florida

Migdalia Schneider
Teacher/Bilingual
Lindell School
Long Beach, New York

Susan Shelly
Teacher
Bonita Springs Elementary
Bonita Springs, Florida

Peggy Terry
Teacher
Madison Elementary
South Holland, Illinois

Jane M. Thompson
Teacher
Emma Ward Elementary
Lawrenceburg, Kentucky

Martha Todd
Teacher
W. H. Rhodes Elementary
Milton, Florida

Renee Williams
Teacher
Bloomfield Schools
Central Primary
Bloomfield, New Mexico

Myra Wood
Teacher
Madison Street Academy
Ocala, Florida

Marion Zampa
Teacher
Shawnee Mission
School District
Overland Park, Kansas

Science

See learning in a whole new light

How to Read Science xx

Science Process Skills xxii

Using Scientific Methods xxvi

Science Tools xxviii

Safety in Science xxxii

v

How do plants live in their habitats?

Chapter 1 • All About Plants

Build Background How do plants live in their habitats? . . . 2

Lab zone **Directed Inquiry Explore** Do plants need water? . . 4

How to Read Science Predict 5

Chapter 1 Song "Plants" 6

Lesson 1 • What are the parts of a plant? 7

Lesson 2 • How are seeds scattered? 10

Lesson 3 • How are plants grouped? 12

Lesson 4 • How are some woodland plants adapted?. . 16

Lesson 5 • How are some prairie plants adapted? . . . 20

Lesson 6 • How are some desert plants adapted? . . . 22

Lesson 7 • How are some marsh plants adapted? . . . 24

Lab zone **Guided Inquiry Investigate** Do plants need light?. 26

Math in Science Leaf Patterns 28

Chapter 1 Review and Test Prep. 30

Biography Mary Agnes Chase 32

Chapter 2 • All About Animals

Build Background How are animals different from each other?. 34

Directed Inquiry **Explore** How are worms and snakes alike and different? 36

How to Read Science **Alike and Different** . . . 37

Chapter 2 Song "What Has Backbones?" 38

Lesson 1 • What are some animals with backbones? . . 39

Lesson 2 • What are some ways mammals are adapted? 42

Lesson 3 • What are some ways birds are adapted? . . 44

Lesson 4 • What are some ways fish are adapted? . . . 46

Lesson 5 • What are some ways reptiles are adapted? . 48

Lesson 6 • What are some ways amphibians are adapted? 50

Lesson 7 • What are some animals without backbones? 52

Guided Inquiry **Investigate** How can an octopus use its arms? 56

Math in Science Sorting Animals. 58

Chapter 2 Review and Test Prep. 60

Life Along the Ice. 62

Career Wildlife Rehabilitator. 64

How are animals different from each other?

Unit A Life Science

Chapter 3 • How Plants and Animals Live Together

How do living things help each other?

Build Background How do living things help each
other?. 66

Lab zone Directed Inquiry Explore What does yeast need
to grow?. 68

How to Read Science Cause and Effect 69

Chapter 3 Song "Good Partners" 70

Lesson 1 • What do plants and animals need? 71

Lesson 2 • How do plants and animals get food in a
grassland? 74

Lesson 3 • How do plants and animals get food in
an ocean?. 78

Lesson 4 • What can cause a food web to change? . . 82

Lesson 5 • How do plants and animals help each other? 84

Lab zone Guided Inquiry Investigate How can you model
a food web?. 90

Math in Science Measuring Length. 92

Chapter 3 Review and Test Prep. 94

Career Farmer 96

Chapter 4 • How Living Things Grow and Change

Build Background How do living things grow in different ways? 98

Lab zone **Directed Inquiry Explore** Which hand do different children use to write? 100

How to Read Science Infer 101

Chapter 4 Song "Hi Little Turtle!" 102

Lesson 1 • How do sea turtles grow and change? . . 103

Lesson 2 • What is the life cycle of a dragonfly? . . . 108

Lesson 3 • What is the life cycle of a horse? 110

Lesson 4 • How are young animals like their parents? 112

Lesson 5 • What is the life cycle of a bean plant? . . 114

Lesson 6 • How are young plants like their parents? . 116

Lesson 7 • How do people grow and change? 118

Lab zone **Guided Activity Investigate** How does a caterpillar grow and change? 122

Math in Science Measuring Time 124

Chapter 4 Review and Test Prep 126

NASA Biography Mario J. Mota 128

Unit A Test Talk 129

Unit A Wrap-Up 130

Lab zone **Full Inquiry Experiment** Which bird beak can crush seeds? 132

End with a Poem "Little Seeds" 134

Science Fair Projects: Temperature and Seeds; Jumping Insects 136

How do living things grow in different ways?

Unit B Earth Science

What are Earth's natural resources?

Chapter 5 • Earth's Land, Air, and Water

Build Background What are Earth's natural resources? . . 138

Lab zone **Directed Inquiry Explore** How are soils different? 140

How to Read Science Picture Clues 141

Chapter 5 Song "Natural Resources" 142

Lesson 1 • What are natural resources? 143

Lesson 2 • What are rocks and soil like?. 146

Lesson 3 • How do people use plants?. 150

Lesson 4 • How does Earth change?. 152

Lesson 5 • How can people help protect Earth? . . . 154

Lab zone **Guided Inquiry Investigate** How do worms change the soil? 160

Math in Science Recycling Bar Graph 162

Chapter 5 Review and Test Prep. 164

NASA Looking out for Earth 166

Career Forester 168

Chapter 6 • Earth's Weather and Seasons

Build Background How does weather change? 170

Lab zone **Directed Inquiry Explore** How much rain falls? . 172

How to Read Science Draw Conclusions. . . 173

Chapter 6 Song "What's the Weather?" 174

Lesson 1 • What are some kinds of weather? 175

Lesson 2 • What is the water cycle? 178

Lesson 3 • What is spring? 180

Lesson 4 • What is summer? 182

Lesson 5 • What is fall? 184

Lesson 6 • What is winter? 186

Lesson 7 • What are some kinds of bad weather? . . 188

Lab zone **Guided Inquiry Investigate** How can you
measure weather changes? 194

Math in Science Charting Favorite Seasons. 196

Chapter 6 Review and Test Prep. 198

Career Atmospheric Scientist. 200

How does weather change?

How can people learn about the Earth long ago?

Chapter 7 • Fossils and Dinosaurs

Build Background How can people learn about the Earth long ago?. 202

Directed Inquiry Explore Which fossils match the plants and animals?. 204

How to Read Science Retell. 205

Chapter 7 Song "Go Find A Fossil" 206

Lesson 1 • How can we learn about the past? 207

Lesson 2 • What can we learn from fossils? 210

Lesson 3 • What were dinosaurs like? 212

Lesson 4 • What are some new discoveries?. 216

Guided Inquiry Investigate How can you make a model of a fossil?. 218

Math in Science Measuring Fossil Leaves. 220

Chapter 7 Review and Test Prep. 222

Biography Susan Hendrickson. 224

Unit B Test Talk 225

Unit B Wrap-Up 226

Full Inquiry Experiment Does gravel, sand, or soil make the best imprint? 228

End with a Poem "The Spring Wind". 230

Science Fair Projects: Water Evaporates; Measuring Temperature. 232

STEM Project Compost Gold EM2

What are some properties of matter?

Chapter 8 • Properties of Matter

Build Background What are some properties of matter? . 234

Lab zone **Directed Inquiry Explore** What happens when oil is mixed with water? 236

How to Read Science Draw Conclusions. . . 237

Chapter 8 Song "They're All Matter" 238

Lesson 1 • What is matter? 239

Lesson 2 • What are the states of matter? 242

Lesson 3 • How can matter be changed? 248

Lesson 4 • How can cooling and heating change matter? 252

Lab zone **Guided Inquiry Investigate** How can water change? 256

Math in Science How Can You Measure Matter? . . . 258

Chapter 8 Review and Test Prep 260

NASA Space Food 262

NASA **Career** Material Scientist. 264

Chapter 9 • Energy

Build Background What are some kinds of energy? . . . 266

Lab zone **Directed Inquiry Explore** Which color heats faster? 268

How to Read Science Infer 269

Chapter 9 Song "Where Do We Get Energy?" 270

Lesson 1 • What is energy? 271

Lesson 2 • How do living things use energy? 274

Lesson 3 • What are some sources of heat? 278

Lesson 4 • How does light move? 282

Lesson 5 • What are other kinds of energy? 286

Lab zone **Guided Inquiry Investigate** How can you change light? 290

Math in Science Measuring Shadows 292

Chapter 9 Review and Test Prep 294

Career Lighting Operator 296

What are some kinds of energy?

Unit C — Physical Science

How do forces cause objects to move?

Chapter 10 • Forces and Motion

Build Background How do forces cause objects to move? 298

Lab zone **Directed Inquiry Explore** How can you measure force?. 300

How to Read Science Put Things in Order . . 301

Chapter 10 Song "Use Some Force!" 302

Lesson 1 • How do objects move?. 303

Lesson 2 • What is work?. 308

Lesson 3 • How can you change the way things move? 310

Lesson 4 • How can simple machines help you do work? 314

Lesson 5 • What are magnets? 318

Lab zone **Guided Inquiry Investigate** What can magnets do? 322

Math in Science Measuring Motion 324

Chapter 10 Review and Test Prep 326

NASA Biography Luther Jenkins 328

Chapter 11 • Sound

Build Background How is sound made?. 330

Lab zone **Directed Inquiry Explore** How can you make sound? 332

How to Read Science Important Details . . . 333

Chapter 11 Song "Listen to the Sounds!" 334

Lesson 1 • What is sound? 335

Lesson 2 • What is pitch?. 338

Lesson 3 • How does sound travel? 340

Lesson 4 • How do some animals make sounds? . . . 342

Lesson 5 • What are some sounds around you? . . . 344

Lab zone **Guided Inquiry Investigate** How can you change sound? 346

Math in Science Measuring Sounds 348

Chapter 11 Review and Test Prep 350

Biography Alejandro Purgue 352

Unit C Test Talk 353

Unit C Wrap-Up 354

Lab zone **Full Inquiry Experiment** What kinds of objects reflect light clearly? 356

End with a Poem "Apple Shadows" 358

Science Fair Projects: Energy in My Terrarium; Listening to Sound Through Matter. 360

STEM Project The Inclined Plane EM6

How is sound made?

Unit D   Space and Technology

What are some ways the Earth moves?

Chapter 12 • Earth and Space

Build Background What are some ways the Earth moves? 362

Directed Inquiry Explore What causes day and night? 364

How to Read Science Alike and Different . . 365

Chapter 12 Song "The Sun" 366

Lesson 1 • What is the Sun? 367

Lesson 2 • What causes day and night? 370

Lesson 3 • What causes seasons to change? 374

Lesson 4 • What can you see in the night sky? . . . 376

Lesson 5 • Why does the Moon seem to change? . . 380

Lesson 6 • What is the solar system? 382

Guided Inquiry Investigate How can you make a model of a constellation? 384

Math in Science Planets in Orbit 386

Chapter 12 Review and Test Prep 388

NASA Mission to Mars 390

NASA Career Astronomer 392

Chapter 13 • Technology in Our World

Build Background What are some ways technology helps us? 394

Lab zone **Directed Inquiry Explore** How can you move the ball? 396

How to Read Science Retell 397

Chapter 13 Song "Technology Helps Us All" 398

Lesson 1 • What is technology? 399

Lesson 2 • How does technology help us? 402

Lesson 3 • How do we use technology to communicate? 404

Lesson 4 • What are some other ways we use technology? 406

Lesson 5 • How do people make things? 408

Lab zone **Guided Inquiry Investigate** How can you make a maze? 410

Math in Science Technology in Your School 412

Chapter 13 Review and Test Prep 414

NASA **Biography** Shonte Wright 416

Unit D Test Talk 417

Unit D Wrap-Up 418

Lab zone **Full Inquiry Experiment** Which tissue is the strongest? 420

End with a Poem "This Happy Day" 422

Science Fair Projects: Phases of the Moon; Flying Better 424

Metric and Customary Measurement EM1
STEM EM2
Glossary/Glosario EM10
Index EM53
Credits EM61

What are some ways technology helps us?

How to Read Science

Each chapter in your book has a page like this one. This page shows you how to use a reading skill.

Before reading
First, read the Build Background page. Next, read the How To Read Science page. Then, think about what you already know. Last, make a list of what you already know.

Target Reading Skill
Each page has a target reading skill. The target reading skill will help you understand what you read.

Real-World Connection
Each page has an example of something you will learn.

Graphic Organizer
A graphic organizer can help you think about what you learn.

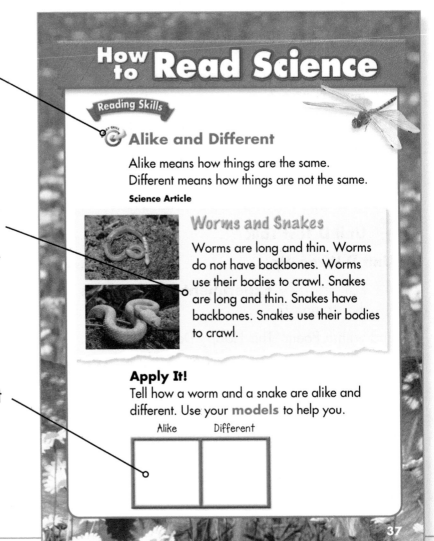

How to Read Science

Reading Skills

Alike and Different

Alike means how things are the same. Different means how things are not the same.

Science Article

Worms and Snakes

Worms are long and thin. Worms do not have backbones. Worms use their bodies to crawl. Snakes are long and thin. Snakes have backbones. Snakes use their bodies to crawl.

Apply It!
Tell how a worm and a snake are alike and different. Use your **models** to help you.

Alike	Different

37

Reptiles are animals with backbones. Most reptiles have dry skin. Scales cover and protect a reptile's body. Some reptiles hatch from eggs. Snakes and turtles are two kinds of reptiles. Look at the picture of the reptile.

Amphibians are animals with backbones. Amphibians live part of their life in the water and part of their life on land. Most amphibians have smooth, wet skin. Amphibians hatch from eggs. Frogs and toads are amphibians.

✓ Lesson Checkpoint

1. Which kinds of animals have backbones and scales?

2. How are an amphibian and a reptile **alike** and **different?**

amphibian

reptile

41

Process Skills

10. **Communicate** Choose an animal in this chapter. Tell one way the animal is adapted to its environment.

Alike and Different

11. Tell how a spider and an insect are **alike and different.**

Alike	Different

Test Prep

Fill in the circle next to the correct answer.

12. Which kind of animal has feathers and wings?
    Ⓐ fish
    Ⓑ bird
    Ⓒ mammal
    Ⓓ amphibian

13. **Writing in Science** Choose an animal. Tell how the animal is adapted to its environment.

61

During reading

Use the checkpoint as you read the lesson. This will help you check how much you understand.

After reading

Think about what you have learned. Compare what you learned with the list you made before you read the chapter. Answer the questions in the Chapter Review.

Target Reading Skills

These are some target reading skills that appear in this book.

- Cause and Effect
- Alike and Different
- Put Things in Order
- Predict

- Draw Conclusions
- Picture Clues
- Important Details

Science Process Skills

Scientists use process skills to find out about things. You will use these skills when you do the activities in this book. Suppose scientists want to learn more about space. Which process skills might they use?

Observe

A scientist who wants to find out more about space observes many things. You use your senses to find out about things too.

Classify

Scientists classify objects in space. You classify when you sort or group things by their properties.

Estimate and Measure

Scientists build machines to explore space. First scientists make a careful guess about the size or amount of the parts of the machine. Then they measure each part.

Infer

Scientists are always learning about space. Scientists draw a conclusion or make a guess from what they already know.

Space

Predict
First scientists tell what they think will happen. Then they do an experiment.

Make and Use Models
Scientists might make and use models of a machine to use in space. Models show what scientists already know.

Make Definitions
Scientists use what they know to tell what something means.

Science Process Skills

Suppose you were a scientist. You might want to learn more about space. What questions might you have? How would you use process skills to help you learn?

Make Hypotheses
Think of a question you have about space. Make a statement that you can test to answer your question.

Collect Data
Scientists record what they observe and measure. Scientists put this data into charts or graphs.

Interpret Data
Scientists use what they learn to solve problems or answer questions.

Investigate and Experiment

Scientists plan a fair test. Scientists change only one thing in their test. Scientists keep everything else the same.

Control Variables

Scientists plan and do an investigation as they study space.

Communicate

Scientists tell what they learn about space.

Using Scientific Methods

Scientific methods are ways of finding answers. Scientific methods have these steps. Sometimes scientists do the steps in a different order. Scientists do not always do all of the steps.

Ask a question.

Ask a question that you want answered.

Do seeds need water to grow?

Make your hypothesis.

Tell what you think the answer is to your question.

If seeds are watered, then they will grow.

Plan a fair test.

Change only one thing.

Keep everything else the same.

Water one pot with seeds.

no water

water

Do your test.

Test your hypothesis. Do your test more than once. See if your results are the same.

Collect and record your data.

Keep records of what you find out. Use words or drawings to help.

Tell your conclusion.

Observe the results of your test. Decide if your hypothesis is right or wrong. Tell what you decide.

Seeds need water to grow.

no water

water

Go further.

Use what you learn. Think of new questions or better ways to do a test.

Ask a Question

Make Your Hypothesis

Plan a Fair Test

Do Your Test

Collect and Record Your Data

Tell Your Conclusion

Go Further

Science Tools

Scientists use many different kinds of tools.

Safety goggles
You can use safety goggles to protect your eyes.

Hand lens
A hand lens makes objects look larger.

Clock
A clock measures time.

Magnet
You can use a magnet to see if an object is made of certain metals.

Stopwatch
A stopwatch measures how long something takes.

Ruler
You can use a ruler to measure how long something is. Most scientists use a ruler to measure length in centimeters or millimeters.

Science Tools

Meterstick
You can use a meterstick to measure how long something is too. Scientists use a meterstick to measure in meters.

Balance
A balance is used to measure the mass of objects. Mass is how much matter an object has. Most scientists measure mass in grams or kilograms.

Measuring cup
You can use a measuring cup to measure volume. Volume is how much space something takes up.

Calculator
A calculator can help you do number problems, such as adding and subtracting.

Thermometer
A thermometer measures the temperature. When the temperature gets warmer, the red line moves up. When it gets cooler, the red line moves down. Most thermometers have a Celsius and Fahrenheit scale. Most scientists use the Celsius scale.

Computer
You can learn about science at a special Internet website. Go to www.pearsonsuccessnet.com.

Safety in Science

You need to be careful when doing science activities. This page includes safety tips to remember:

- Listen to your teacher's instructions.
- Never taste or smell materials unless your teacher tells you to.
- Wear safety goggles when needed.
- Handle scissors and other equipment carefully.
- Keep your work place neat and clean.
- Clean up spills immediately.
- Tell your teacher immediately about accidents or if you see something that looks unsafe.
- Wash your hands well after every activity.

Unit A

Life Science

Unit A

Chapter 1 All About Plants

Directed Inquiry — Do plants need water?

Guided Inquiry — Do plants need light?

Activity Flip Chart — What are the parts of a flowering plant?
How are a cactus and a fern alike and different?

Quick Activity Transparencies — How are these plants alike?
How do plant seeds travel?
Can you find the seeds in each fruit?
What are the four seasons?
What is a prairie like?
What is a desert like?
What is a marsh or wetland like?

Chapter 2 All About Animals

Directed Inquiry — How are worms and snakes alike and different?

Guided Inquiry — How can an octopus use its arms?

Activity Flip Chart — How does camouflage help an animal survive?
Why does a backbone have many parts?

Quick Activity Transparencies — How are animals alike and different?
What animal is a mammal?
How are tools used for eating?
How does an animal protect itself?
How are these reptiles alike?
Where are frogs found?
What kinds of insects do you know?

Chapter 3 How Plants and Animals Live Together

Directed Inquiry — What does yeast need to grow?

Guided Inquiry — How can you model a food web?

Activity Flip Chart — What is a food chain?
How does a bird make a nest?

Quick Activity Transparencies — What do you need to live and grow?
What do animals eat?
How do plants and animals get food in an ocean?
What can hurt a food web?
How can plants help animals with shelter?

Chapter 4 How Living Things Grow and Change

Directed Inquiry — Which hand do different children use to write?

Guided Inquiry — How does a caterpillar grow and change?

Activity Flip Chart — How common are some traits?
What happens when a seed germinates?

Quick Activity Transparencies — What do sea turtles need to live?
Which of these insects is a dragonfly?
Is a horse a mammal?
Do young animals look like their parents?
How does a bean plant change and grow?
How are young plants like their parents?
How do people grow and change?

Unit A

Full Inquiry — Which bird beak can crush seeds?

You Will Discover

- how each part of a plant helps the plant live.
- where different kinds of plants live.

Chapter 1
All About
Plants

online
Student Edition
pearsonsuccessnet.com

How do plants live in their habitats?

stem

flower

nutrients

Nutrients are materials that living things need to live and grow.

roots

2

environment

Chapter 1 Vocabulary

nutrients page 7

roots page 8

stem page 8

leaves page 8

flower page 9

environment page 16

adapted page 16

prairie page 20

leaves

adapted

prairie

Explore Do plants need water?

Materials

celery

jar

water

What to Do

1 Put celery in the jar.
Look at the celery.

2 Wait 1 day.
How did the celery
change?

3 Put water in the jar.
Predict what
will happen
to the celery.

4 Wait 1 day. How did the
celery change? Why did it change?

Explain Your Results
Predict What will happen if you
take the celery out of the water?

Process Skills

You **predict**
when you tell
what you think
might happen.

How to Read Science

TARGET SKILL

Predict

Predict means to tell what you think might happen next.

Science Story

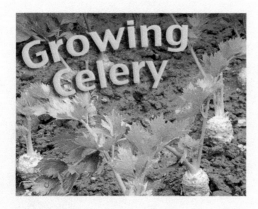

Growing Celery

Workers plant celery seeds in little pots. When the seeds begin to grow, farmers move the young plants to fields. The farmers cut the celery when it is grown.

Apply It!

Predict what will happen to the celery next. Make a graphic organizer to help you.

I Know   I Predict

♪ **Plants**

Sung to the tune of "Where, Oh, Where Has My Little Dog Gone?"
Lyrics by Gerri Brioso & Richard Freitas/The Dovetail Group, Inc.

Plants have roots that grow in soil,
And hold the plant in place.
The roots take in water and nutrients,
And carry them up to the stem.

Lesson 1

What are the parts of a plant?

Plants need water, air, and sunlight. Plants need space to grow. Plants need nutrients. **Nutrients** are materials that living things need to live and grow. Many plants get nutrients from soil and water.

The parts of a plant help it get food, water, air, and sunlight.

Plant Parts

Plants have different parts. The four main parts are the roots, stem, leaves, and flowers.

Roots grow down into the soil. Roots hold the plant in place. Roots take water and nutrients from the soil to the stem.

The **stem** carries water and nutrients to the leaves. The stem holds up the plant.

Green **leaves** take in sunlight and air. They use sunlight, air, water, and nutrients to make food for the plant.

Leaves

Roots

Many plants have flowers. A **flower** makes seeds. These seeds might grow into new plants.

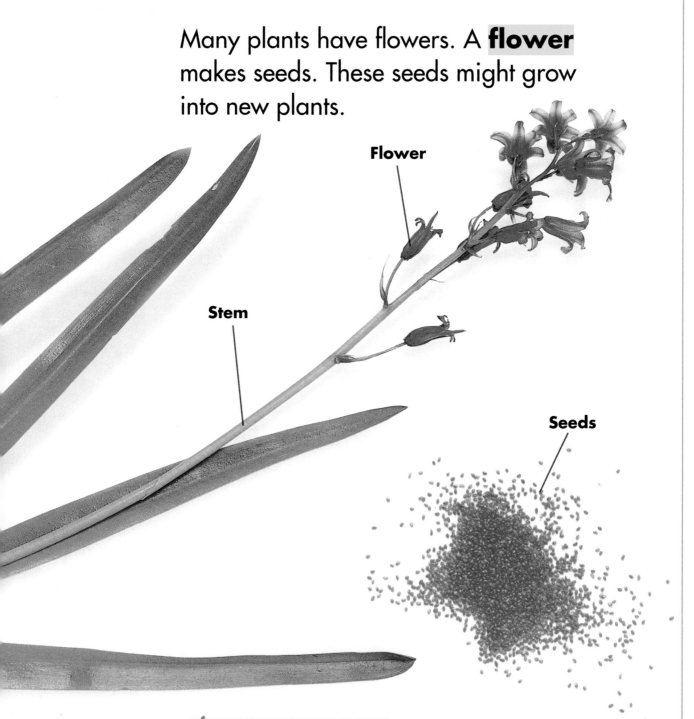

Flower

Stem

Seeds

✔ Lesson Checkpoint

1. What are the four main parts of a plant?

2. **Writing** in Science

Write a sentence in your journal. Tell why the stem of a plant is important.

Lesson 2

How are seeds scattered?

Many new plants grow from seeds. Suppose you plant seeds. You would scatter the seeds in the soil. Scatter means to spread out. The seeds have space to grow.

Fruits cover and protect seeds. When fruits travel, the seeds inside are scattered. Some fruits are scattered by air or water. Some fruits get stuck on the fur or feathers of animals. Scattering helps carry seeds to new places where they might grow.

✔ **Lesson Checkpoint**

1. Name 3 ways that seeds travel.

2. 🔄 **Predict** A maple tree fruit spins to the ground. It lands in an open field. What do you think might happen next?

The fruits of a maple tree are shaped like wings. This shape helps them travel through the air.

The fruits of the water lily float on lakes and streams.

Burrs are fruits. Burrs travel by sticking on clothing or fur. This dog has burrs stuck to its fur.

How are plants grouped?

Plants can be grouped into two kinds. One kind of plant has flowers. The other kind of plant does not have flowers.

Plants with flowers grow in different places. Trees are plants. Some trees have flowers. The flowers form fruits that cover and protect the seeds inside.

Peach trees grow flowers. Peaches are a fruit. You can eat peaches.

Cactus plants grow in the desert. Their flowers form seeds. Some seeds fall into the sand. New cactus plants might grow.

Saguaro cactus flowers open during cool nights.

1. ✓Checkpoint How are plants grouped?

2. Health in Science Name some fruits that you can eat.

Plants Without Flowers

Not all plants have flowers. Some plants have cones. Seeds grow inside the cones. When a cone opens, the seeds fall out. Some seeds grow into new trees.

Mosses are tiny plants that do not have flowers. Mosses do not make seeds or fruits. Mosses do not have leaves, roots, or stems.

Ferns do not have flowers. Ferns do not make seeds. Ferns have leaves, roots, and stems.

✓ **Lesson Checkpoint**

1. What grows inside cones?

2. **Art** in Science Draw a forest. Label trees, mosses, and ferns.

Pine trees
have cones.

Mosses often
grow on wet
rocks.

Some ferns
live in warm,
shady, wet
places.

15

Lesson 4

How are some woodland plants adapted?

Plants live almost everywhere. A plant's **environment** is all the living and nonliving things around it.

Living things have **adapted,** or changed, to live in their environment.

Many kinds of plants grow in a woodland environment. Pine trees are adapted to live in cold weather. Pine trees have small leaves that are shaped like needles.

Pine tree leaves are adapted to keep from drying out in cold weather.

SciLinks Take It to the Net
pearsonsuccessnet.com   keyword: environment
code: g2p16

Maple tree leaves turn color in the fall.

Maple trees are adapted to live where summers are warm and winters are cold. Maple trees have large flat leaves. The maple tree loses its leaves in winter. This helps the tree keep the water it needs to live in winter.

1. ✔ **Checkpoint** How are pine trees adapted to their environment?

2. **Math** in Science Find a leaf outside. Use paper clips and counters to measure it.

Plants That Live Near Water

Some plants in a woodland environment live near rivers and streams.

Plants that grow near rivers and streams are adapted to live where it is very wet.

This red plant is called a cardinal plant. The roots of a cardinal plant are adapted to get nutrients from the moist soil in a woodland.

Cardinal plant

☑ **Lesson Checkpoint**

1. How is a fanwort adapted to its wet habitat?

2. **Social Studies** in Science
Look at a map. Find a river or stream in your state.

The stinging nettle has tiny, sharp hairs on its stem. The hairs protect the plant from animals that want to eat it.

The fanwort is adapted to live in water. Water can move through the thin leaves of the plant.

19

How are some prairie plants adapted?

A **prairie** is flat land with lots of grass and few trees. Many prairies have hot summers with little rain. Some prairie plants are adapted to keep water when there is not enough rain.

Goldenrod plants have stiff stems and leaves. The stems and leaves help the plants keep the water they need to live.

Goldenrod

✓ Lesson Checkpoint

1. How are goldenrod plants adapted?

2. **Writing** in Science Write a sentence in your **science journal.** Tell how prairie plants are different from woodland plants.

Prairie smoke has fuzz on its stems and leaves. The fuzz helps the plant keep the water it needs.

Prairie grasses have thin leaves. The leaves help the plants keep the water they need.

How are some desert plants adapted?

Many deserts are sunny and hot during the day. Deserts can be cool at night. Very little rain falls in a desert environment.

Some desert plants are adapted to hold water for a long time. The desert almond has leaves that grow in different directions. Some leaves get less sunlight than others. Leaves that get less sunlight can keep the water they need to live.

Desert almond

✔ **Lesson Checkpoint**

1. Tell about the leaves of a desert almond.

2. **Social Studies** in Science
   Find Arizona on a map. Name a desert in Arizona.

The saguaro cactus has a long, thick stem that holds water.

The octopus tree has long spines. The spines protect the plant from animals that want to eat the leaves.

Lesson 7

How are some marsh plants adapted?

A marsh is an environment that is very wet. The soil in a marsh may not have the nutrients plants need. The plants in a marsh are adapted to get nutrients in other ways.

Cattails are plants. Cattails are adapted to grow in very wet soil. Cattails get the nutrients they need from the water.

Cattails

✓ Lesson Checkpoint

1. How does a sundew plant trap insects?

2. **Predict** An insect lands on the leaf of a Venus's-flytrap. Predict what will happen next.

A sundew plant gets some nutrients from insects. The plant has sticky hairs on each leaf. Insects land on a leaf and stick to the hairs.

A Venus's-flytrap also gets some nutrients from insects. An insect lands on the plant's leaves. Then the leaves snap shut.

Investigate Do plants need light?

Plants need water, air, sunlight, and nutrients to live and grow. What might happen if plants do not get light?

Materials

2 cups with grass

water

What to Do

1 Water both plants.

You can paint your cups!

2 Put one plant in sunlight.

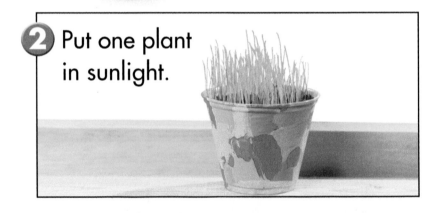

3 Put the other plant in a dark place.

Process Skills

You **observe** when you look closely at the plants.

4 How do you think the plants will look after 1 week? **Observe** the plants every day for 1 week.

	Sunlight	Dark
Day 1		
Day 2		

5 Fill in the chart. Draw pictures to show the plants each day.

Explain Your Results

1. Which plant grew better?
2. **Infer** What will happen if a plant does not get sunlight?

Go Further

What will happen if you move the plant from the dark place to a sunny place? Try it and find out.

Leaf Patterns

Ash tree leaves

Leaves grow on branches in different patterns. Ash tree leaves grow in pairs. Two leaves grow across from each other. One leaf is on one side of a stalk. One leaf is on the other side.

Beech tree leaves grow in a different pattern. One leaf grows on one side of a stalk. Farther down, another leaf grows on the other side of the branch. This pattern repeats.

Beech tree leaves

Copy the leaf pictures below. Use what you know about leaf patterns. Predict where the next two leaves will grow. Draw two more leaves on each stalk.

Vocabulary

Which picture goes with each word?

1. stem
2. leaf
3. flowers
4. prairie
5. roots

What did you learn?

6. What are nutrients?
7. What is a plant's environment?
8. How is prairie smoke adapted to live on a prairie?

9. **Infer** What might happen if a plant does not get enough space to live and grow?

Predict

10. The leaves on a maple tree change color from green to red. **Predict** what will happen next.

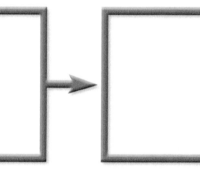

I Know → I Predict

Test Prep

Fill in the circle next to the correct answer.

11. Which part of a plant brings water up to the leaves?

Ⓐ stem

Ⓑ cone

Ⓒ roots

Ⓓ flower

12. **Writing in Science** Name the 4 main parts of a plant. Tell how each part helps the plant.

Mary Agnes Chase

Read Together

Mary Agnes Chase was born in 1869. She liked to collect plants when she was young. She drew pictures of the plants.

When she was older, Mary Agnes Chase became a plant scientist. She went all over the world studying plants. She kept drawing pictures of all the different plants.

Mary Agnes Chase wrote books to help other people learn about plants. Her drawings were in her books.

Lab zone Take-Home Activity

Find a grass plant or other plant growing outside. Draw a picture of it. Talk to your family about your drawing.

You Will Discover

- that there are many different kinds of animals.
- how animals are adapted to different kinds of environments.

Chapter 2
All About
Animals

Web Games
Take It to the Net
pearsonsuccessnet.com

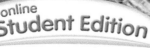

online
Student Edition
pearsonsuccessnet.com

How are animals different from each other?

mammal

bird

fish gills

34

Chapter 2
Vocabulary

mammal page 40

bird page 40

fish page 40

reptile page 41

amphibian page 41

camouflage page 42

gills page 46

insect page 52

reptile

amphibian

camouflage

insect

Explore How are worms and snakes alike and different?

Materials

short tape

long tape

7 cotton squares

pipe cleaner

14 pieces of pasta

What to Do

Make models of a worm and a snake.

Worm

1 Roll up.
Pinch the ends.

Snake

2 String the pasta.

3 Roll up.
Pinch the ends.

Explain Your Results

Feel the **models**. Tell about them.

How to Read Science

Reading Skills

TARGET SKILL ⟳ Alike and Different

Alike means how things are the same.
Different means how things are not the same.

Science Article

Worms and Snakes

Worms are long and thin. Worms do not have backbones. Worms use their bodies to crawl. Snakes are long and thin. Snakes have backbones. Snakes use their bodies to crawl.

Apply It!

Tell how a worm and a snake are alike and different. Use your **models** to help you.

Alike	Different

♪ What Has Backbones?

Sung to the tune of "There's a Hole In The Bucket"
Lyrics by Gerri Brioso & Richard Freitas/The Dovetail Group, Inc.

There are animals with backbones,
Like mammals.
Yes, mammals.
Dogs and cats,
Skunks and chipmunks,
All have backbones.

What are some animals with backbones?

There are many different kinds of animals. One main group of animals has backbones.

Bones help give an animal shape. Bones can help an animal move. Bones can help protect some body parts of animals.

A skunk has a backbone.

Animals with Backbones

Mammals are animals with backbones.
A mammal usually has hair or fur on its body.
Young mammals get milk from their mother.
Dogs and cats are two kinds of mammals.
The chipmunk in the picture is a mammal.

Birds are animals with backbones. Birds have feathers and wings. Birds hatch from eggs.

Fish are animals with backbones. Fish live in water. Most fish are covered with scales. Fish have fins. Most fish hatch from eggs.

mammal

bird

fish

Reptiles are animals with backbones. Most reptiles have dry skin. Scales cover and protect a reptile's body. Some reptiles hatch from eggs. Snakes and turtles are two kinds of reptiles.

Amphibians are animals with backbones. Amphibians live part of their life in the water and part of their life on land. Most amphibians have smooth, wet skin. Amphibians hatch from eggs. Frogs and toads are amphibians.

✓ **Lesson Checkpoint**

1. Which kinds of animals have backbones and scales?

2. How are an amphibian and a reptile **alike** and **different?**

reptile

amphibian

What are some ways mammals are adapted?

Mammals live almost everywhere in the world. Like plants, mammals have adapted to live in their environment. An animal's environment is all the living and nonliving things around it.

Like many animals, mule deer are adapted to their environment by camouflage. **Camouflage** is a color or shape that makes a plant or animal hard to see.

The mule deer's fur is brown in summer.

In winter, the mule deer's fur turns color. The deer is harder to see in the snow.

42

A flying squirrel is adapted to glide from tree to tree.

A hedgehog sleeps for part of the winter.

Some animals are adapted to act in ways that help them live. Chipmunks store some of the food they find in the summer. They sleep for part of the winter. Chipmunks eat some of the food they store every time they wake up.

✓ **Lesson Checkpoint**

1. How does a mule deer's fur change in winter?

2. **Art** in Science Draw a picture of a mammal that you have seen.

What are some ways birds are adapted?

Many birds are adapted to fly. Wings and feathers help birds fly.

This bird is called a nightjar.

The nightjar lives in fields. Its feathers look like the ground. This camouflage helps the bird hide from animals that might eat it.

Hmmm!
A hummingbird's beak is adapted. A hummingbird uses its beak to drink liquid from flowers.

Most penguins live where it is very cold.

A penguin's top feathers are waterproof. These feathers help keep the penguin dry. Tiny feathers below the top feathers trap air. The trapped air helps keep the penguin warm.

Penguins do not fly. Their wings are adapted for swimming.

✓ **Lesson Checkpoint**

1. How does camouflage protect the nightjar?

2. How are hummingbirds and penguins **alike?** How are they **different?**

What are some ways fish are adapted?

Fish are adapted to life in the water. Fish have gills. **Gills** are body parts that help fish get oxygen from the water. Fish have fins to help them swim.

This porcupine fish is adapted to protect itself. The porcupine fish can make itself big. Sharp spikes stick out from its body when it is big.

Gill   Fin

This tiny porcupine fish can become very big.

Changing shape protects the porcupine fish.

Many catfish live in lakes and rivers. Catfish can swim deep in the water where it is dark. Catfish have feelers that look like whiskers. Feelers help catfish find food.

Long feelers help a catfish find food.

This stingray uses the sharp spike on its tail to protect itself.

√ **Lesson Checkpoint**

1. How do porcupine fish protect themselves?

2. **Math** in Science Some catfish are only 10 centimeters long. Use a ruler. Draw a line 10 centimeters long. Find something in your classroom that is the same length.

What are some ways reptiles are adapted?

Reptiles are adapted to changes in air temperature. A reptile's body is cold when the air is cold. A reptile's body is warm when the air is warm. Reptiles can move quickly when they are warm.

Zap!

A chameleon has a long tongue. The chameleon has a sticky ball at the end of its tongue. Food sticks to this ball.

Open wide!

This snake's mouth is adapted to open very wide. This snake can swallow its food whole.

A desert iguana is adapted to live in the hot, sunny desert. Dark colors get hot in the sun. Light colors stay cooler in the sun. The light skin helps the desert iguana keep cool.

desert iguana

✓ Lesson Checkpoint

1. How is a desert iguana adapted to live in its environment?

2. **Writing** in Science Tell one way some snakes are adapted to get food.

What are some ways amphibians are adapted?

Most amphibians begin their life in the water. Many amphibians move to the land when they are grown. Frogs are amphibians. Frogs often live near water. Smooth, wet skin helps frogs live in moist environments.

These tree frogs have bright red eyes. Other animals want to eat the frogs. The frogs' eyes help scare these animals away.

Toads are amphibians. Toads begin their life in water. Toads move to the land when they are grown. Toads dig deep into the ground when it is very hot. They look for food at night.

Most toads have dry, rough skin.

✓ **Lesson Checkpoint**

1. Name one way a toad and a frog are different.

2. **Writing** in Science Tell how bright red eyes can help a tree frog.

What are some animals without backbones?

One main group of animals has backbones. Another main group of animals does not have backbones. Most kinds of animals do not have bones.

Insects are animals that do not have bones. Insects have three body parts. The body parts are the head, the thorax, and the abdomen. Insects have six legs. Antennae help some insects feel, smell, hear, and taste.

Abdomen

This insect is called a walking stick. Camouflage makes the insect hard to see on a plant.

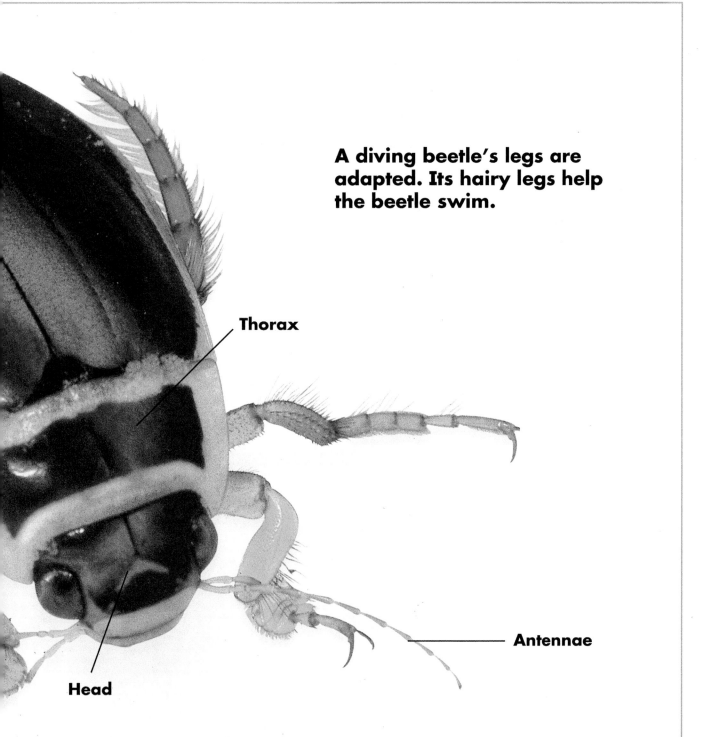

A diving beetle's legs are adapted. Its hairy legs help the beetle swim.

Thorax

Antennae

Head

1. ✓Checkpoint How is the diving beetle adapted to life in water?

2. Technology in Science Tell about inventions that help people move in water.

Other Animals Without Backbones

An octopus lives in the ocean. An octopus is an animal without a backbone.

An octopus is adapted to find and catch food. An octopus has good eyesight. Its eyesight helps it find food. The suction cups on its arms help the octopus hold its food.

An octopus has 8 arms.

Spiders are animals without backbones. Spiders have eight legs. Spiders are adapted to spin webs. The webs trap insects that spiders eat.

This spider builds a web to trap insects.

√ Lesson Checkpoint

1. Tell how the octopus is adapted to find food.

2. **Math** in Science A spider has 8 legs. How many legs will 2 spiders have in all? Write a number sentence to show your answer.

Lab zone Guided Inquiry

Investigate How can an octopus use its arms?

An octopus has suction cups on its 8 arms. It can use its arms to pick things up. Billye the octopus uses its arms to solve a problem. Billye can open a jar to get a fish inside.

Materials

scissors

fish

jar

8 suction cups

What to Do

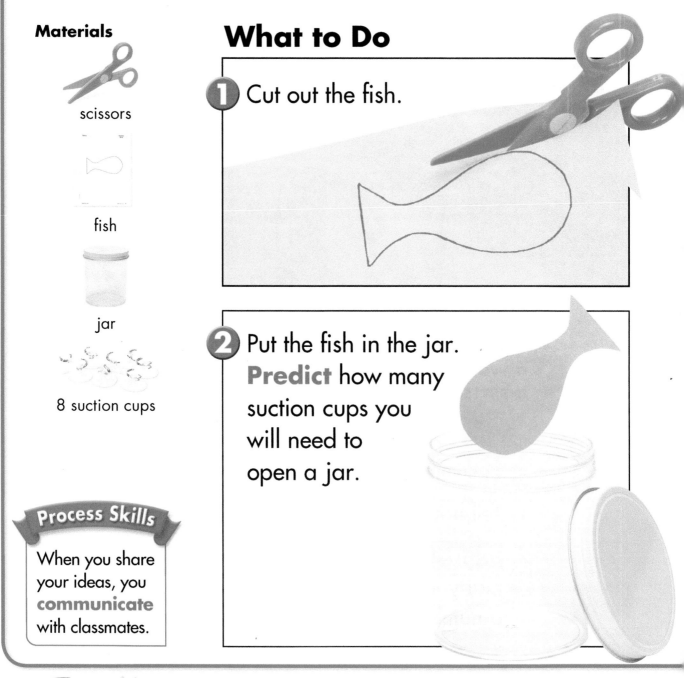

1 Cut out the fish.

2 Put the fish in the jar. **Predict** how many suction cups you will need to open a jar.

More Lab zone Activities Take It to the Net
pearsonsuccessnet.com

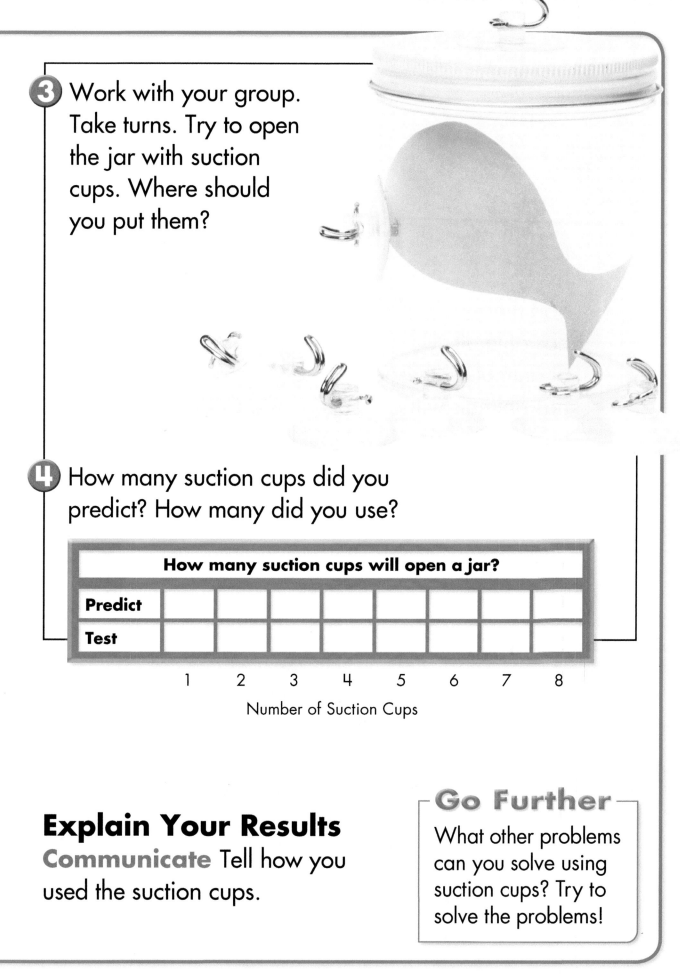

3 Work with your group. Take turns. Try to open the jar with suction cups. Where should you put them?

4 How many suction cups did you predict? How many did you use?

How many suction cups will open a jar?								
Predict								
Test								

1 2 3 4 5 6 7 8

Number of Suction Cups

Explain Your Results
Communicate Tell how you used the suction cups.

Go Further
What other problems can you solve using suction cups? Try to solve the problems!

Math in Science

Sorting Animals

Sort these animals into 2 groups. One group has animals with backbones. Count the number of animals with backbones. The other group has animals without backbones. Count the number of animals without backbones.

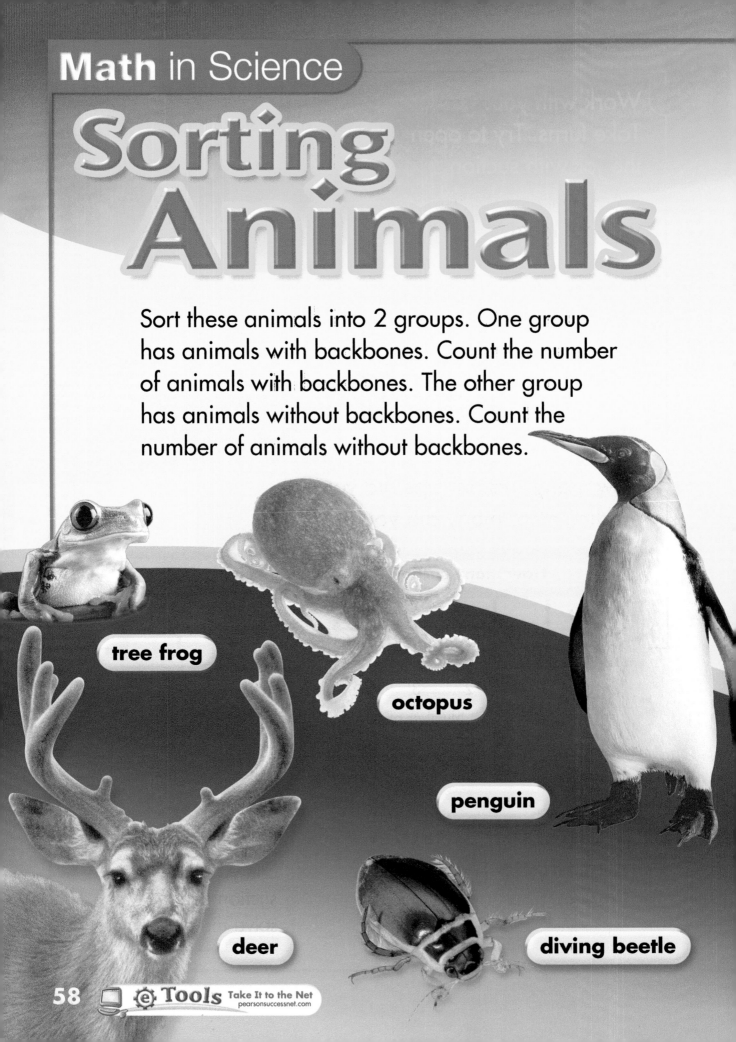

tree frog

octopus

penguin

deer

diving beetle

eTools Take It to the Net
pearsonsuccessnet.com

Make a graph like this one. Color in your graph to show the number of animals in each group.

Animal Groups

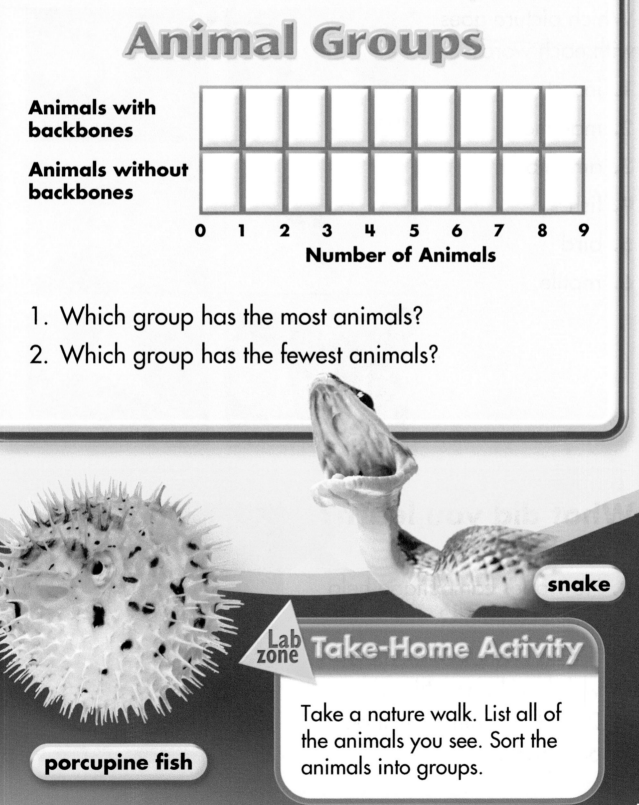

Animals with backbones

Animals without backbones

0 1 2 3 4 5 6 7 8 9

Number of Animals

1. Which group has the most animals?

2. Which group has the fewest animals?

snake

porcupine fish

Lab zone **Take-Home Activity**

Take a nature walk. List all of the animals you see. Sort the animals into groups.

Vocabulary

Which picture goes with each word?

1. insect
2. mammal
3. amphibian
4. fish
5. bird
6. reptile

What did you learn?

7. How do fish use gills?

8. How does camouflage help protect animals?

9. Name 2 kinds of animals with backbones. Name 2 kinds of animals without backbones.

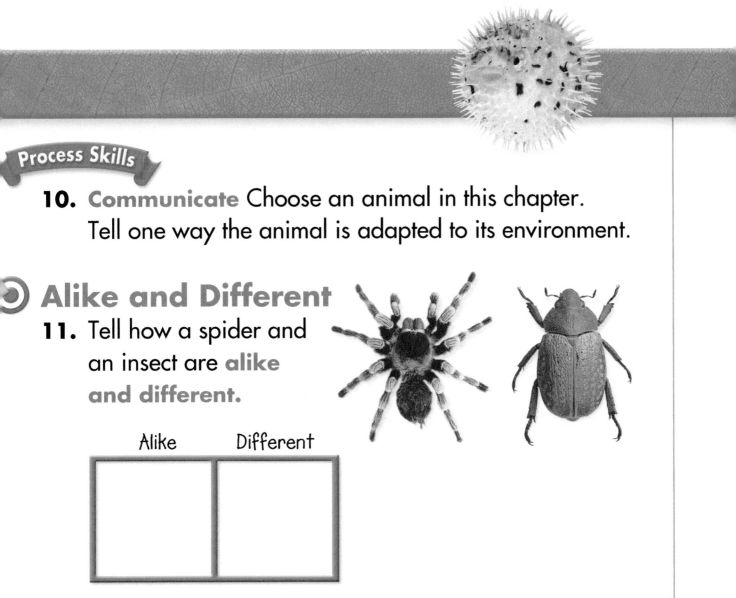

10. **Communicate** Choose an animal in this chapter. Tell one way the animal is adapted to its environment.

Alike and Different

11. Tell how a spider and an insect are **alike and different.**

Alike	Different

Test Prep

Fill in the circle next to the correct answer.

12. Which kind of animal has feathers and wings?

Ⓐ fish

Ⓑ bird

Ⓒ mammal

Ⓓ amphibian

13. **Writing** in Science Choose an animal. Tell how the animal is adapted to its environment.

Life Along the Ice

Scientists working with NASA use satellites to study animals and their environments. Scientists use satellites to learn about penguins that live near Antarctica.

Antarctica is very cold. Most of the ocean water near Antarctica is full of ice. The wind blows holes in the ice. Plants called algae can grow in the holes in the ice. Tiny animals called krill eat the algae. Penguins eat krill.

Scientists have learned that when there are more algae, there are more krill. When there are more krill, there are more penguins. When there are fewer krill, there are fewer penguins.

Krill

Satellites send information about the ocean back to Earth.

Lab zone Take-Home Activity

Draw a picture of a penguin. Tell your family how scientists learn about the ocean. Tell them how the amount of krill affects the number of penguins.

Wildlife Rehabilitator

Read Together

What happens when animals that live in forests or oceans are hurt? Are there ways people can help?

Wildlife rehabilitators are people that help hurt or sick animals. They know what animals need to live in their environment. A wildlife rehabilitator can even teach young animals how to hunt for food.

Wildlife rehabilitators know that it is important that animals get the care they need to survive.

A wildlife rehabilitator saved this sea turtle.

Lab zone Take-Home Activity

Write about what it would be like to be a wildlife rehabilitator. What kinds of animals would you like to help?

You Will Discover

- what plants and animals need.
- how animals depend on plants and other animals.

Chapter 3

How Plants and Animals Live Together

online
Student Edition
pearsonsuccessnet.com

How do living things help each other?

producer

consumer

predator

prey

Chapter 3 Vocabulary

producer page 71

consumer page 71

food chain page 74

predator page 75

prey page 75

food web page 76

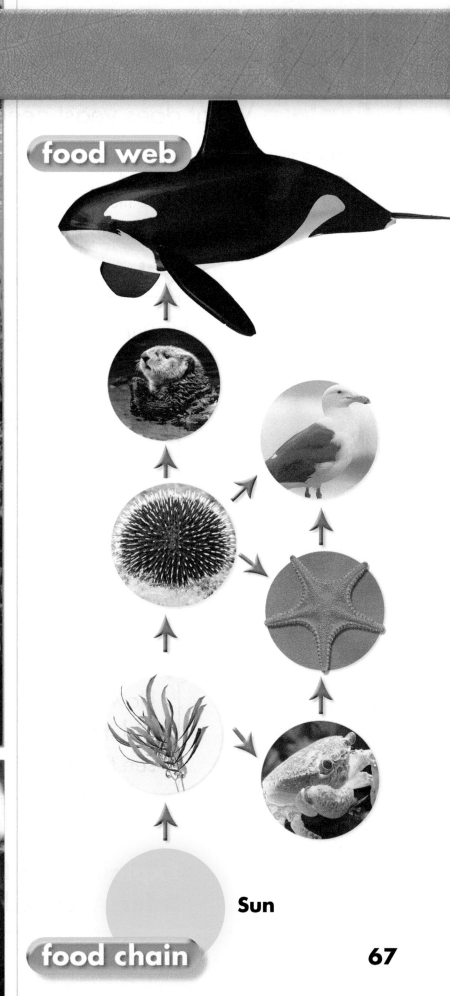

food web

Sun

food chain

Explore What does yeast need to grow?

Yeast are tiny living things.
They cannot make their own food.
They must get food from where they live.

Be careful! Don't slip! Clean up spills.

Materials

cup with yeast

cup with warm water

cup with sugar

spoon

Process Skills

You can **infer** from what you observe with your senses.

What to Do

1 Put water in the cup with yeast.

2 Add sugar and stir. Watch the yeast.

Look at the tiny bubbles!

3 **Estimate** How long did it take to see tiny bubbles?

Explain Your Results

Infer What made the yeast change?

How to Read Science

Cause and Effect

A cause is why something happens.
An effect is what happens.

Science Activity

Yeast is added to bread dough. The yeast causes air bubbles to form in the bread dough. The air bubbles make the bread dough rise.

Apply It!

Infer What would happen to the bread dough without the yeast?

Cause   Effect

Good Partners

Sung to the tune of "Frere Jacques"
Lyrics by Gerri Brioso & Richard Freitas/The Dovetail Group, Inc.

Plants and animals

Are good partners.

Yes they are.

Yes they are.

What do plants and animals need?

You learned that plants need air, water, sunlight, nutrients, and space to grow. Most green plants are producers. A **producer** is a living thing that can make its own food.

Animals need air, water, shelter, and space to live. Animals need food. Animals are consumers. A **consumer** cannot make its own food. Consumers get food from their habitat.

These giraffes are consumers.

71

Different Needs

Many plants and animals live together in a habitat. Plants and animals depend on each other and their habitat to meet their needs.

Large animals often need a lot of food, water, and space. Large animals need a large shelter. Small animals often do not need as much to eat and drink as large animals. Small animals can live in small spaces.

These plants and animals live in the same habitat.

These animals both need water. Which animal do you think needs more water?

Sometimes a habitat does not have enough food for all of the animals that live there. When this happens, some of the animals might die.

✓ **Lesson Checkpoint**

1. What do all animals need?

2. **Cause and Effect** What might happen if there is not enough food for all of the animals in a habitat?

How do plants and animals get food in a grassland?

All living things need food. Most plants make food. Some animals eat plants. Other animals eat those animals. This is called a **food chain.**

Food chains start with the Sun. Plants use energy from the Sun to make food. Animals get energy from the food they eat. Look at the pictures of the food chain. Energy passes from sunlight to the mountain lion.

The corn plant uses water, air, and energy from sunlight to make food.

Crunch! The vole eats the corn for energy.

All food chains have predators and prey. A **predator** is an animal that catches and eats another animal. **Prey** is an animal that is caught and eaten. Look at the animals in the food chain. The coyote and mountain lion are predators. Which animals are their prey?

1. ✔Checkpoint Give an example of a predator and its prey.

2. Art in Science Draw a picture of this grassland food chain. Label your picture.

Pounce! The mountain lion catches and eats the coyote.

Gulp! The coyote eats the vole. The vole is the coyote's prey.

A Food Web in a Grassland

Habitats usually have more than one food chain. The food chains in a habitat make up a **food web.** The plants and animals in a food web need each other for energy.

raccoon

corn plant

vole

fox

These pages show a food web in a grassland. Energy passes from sunlight to the corn. Use your finger to trace how energy moves from the corn to the vole to the fox. This is one food chain. What other food chains can you find on these two pages?

hawk

coyote

mountain lion

✓ **Lesson Checkpoint**

1. Describe a food web.

2. **Math** in Science How many animals in this food web eat the corn? How many animals eat the vole? How many more animals eat the vole than the corn? Write a number sentence.

How do plants and animals get food in an ocean?

An ocean has food chains and food webs too. Many different plants and animals live in an ocean. The pictures on these pages show an ocean food chain.

Kelp grows in an ocean. Kelp uses energy from sunlight to make food.

Sea urchins eat kelp.

Crunch! **A sea star eats the sea urchin.**

Remember that energy is passed through each step in a food chain. Trace how energy in this food chain passes from the Sun to the sea otter.

1. ✔ Checkpoint Where does a sea otter get energy?

2. Writing in Science Write 2 or 3 sentences. Tell how energy moves through this food chain.

Chomp! **The sea otter eats the sea star. The sea otter gets the energy it needs from the sea star.**

A Food Web in an Ocean

Look at this simple ocean food web. Energy passes from sunlight to the kelp. Use your finger to trace the food chains. How many food chains can you count?

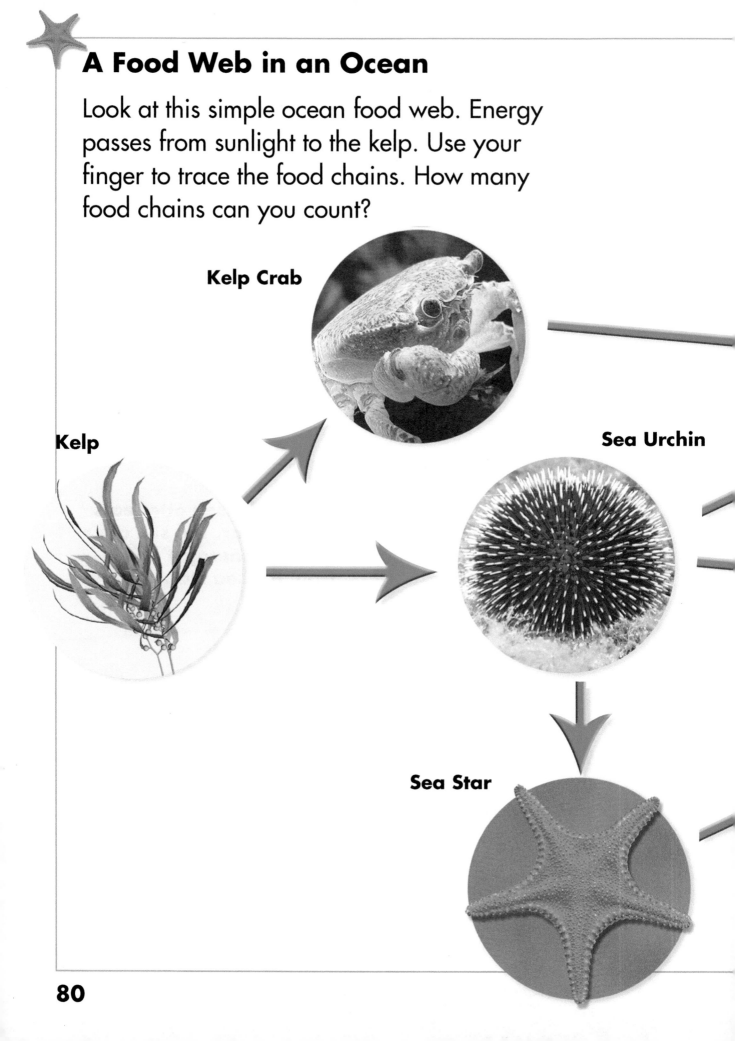

Kelp Crab

Kelp

Sea Urchin

Sea Star

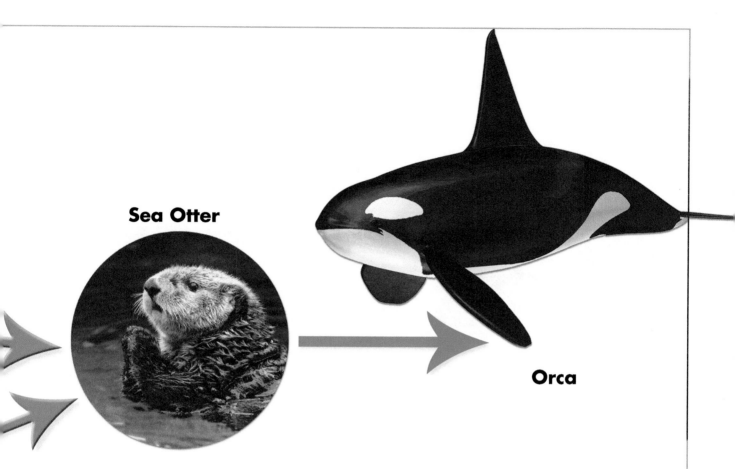

Sea Otter

Orca

Sea Gull

✓**Lesson Checkpoint**

1. What eats kelp in this food web?

2. **Writing** in Science Write one sentence in your journal. Describe one food chain in this ocean food web.

These otters were covered with oil from the oil spill.

This ship had an accident. Oil spilled from the ship into the ocean.

Lesson 4

What can cause a food web to change?

Many things can cause changes in a food web. Some changes may make it hard for plants and animals to survive. Parts of the food web may be harmed or even die.

People can cause a food web to change. The picture shows an oil spill. Many plants and animals were covered with oil.

People washed the oil off of this otter's fur.

People worked together to wash the oil off the animals. People helped to clean the water. People made the water safe again for the plants and animals that live there.

✓ Lesson Checkpoint

1. How did people help after the oil spill?

2. **Cause and Effect** What is one effect of an oil spill?

How do plants and animals help each other?

Sometimes plants and animals help each other. Some animals get shelter from plants. These ants live inside an acacia plant. The ants protect the acacia plant from animals that might eat it.

If other animals try to eat this plant, the ants will bite them on the nose!

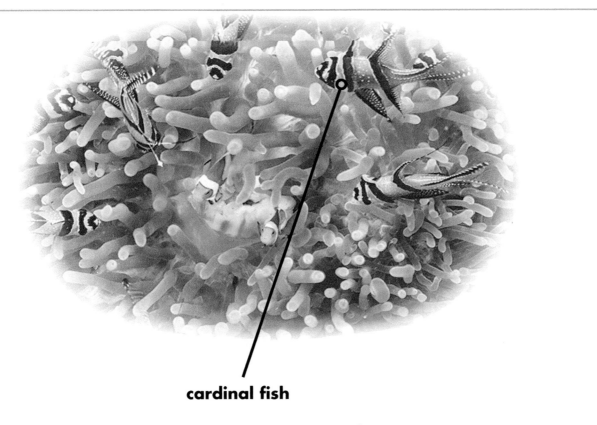

cardinal fish

Some animals get protection from
other animals. Cardinal fish live
near sea urchins. The sharp spines
of the sea urchin protect the fish.
The fish do not help or hurt the
sea urchin.

1. ✓Checkpoint How do ants protect
   an acacia plant?

2. **Social Studies** in Science Acacia
   plants live in Costa Rica. Find Costa
   Rica on a map. You can find it south
   of Florida.

Building Nests

Some animals depend on plants and other animals to build nests. Some animals use parts of plants. Some animals use feathers or fur from other animals to build their nests.

Look at the picture of the squirrel's nest. Twigs and leaves are on the outside of the nest. Dried grass, bark, feathers, and wool are on the inside of the nest.

The masked weaver makes a nest from plant parts.

Some owls that live in the desert build their nests in a cactus.

1. ✓ **Checkpoint** What animal parts does the squirrel use to make its nest?

2. **Writing** in Science Write 2 or 3 sentences in your **science journal.** Tell what you learned about animals that build nests.

Animals Need Each Other

Animals need each other for many reasons. The remora fish in the picture below takes a ride with a blue shark. When the shark eats, the remora fish eats the leftovers! The remora does not hurt or help the shark.

The big shark scares predators away from the little remora.

A bird called an egret sits on top of a rhinoceros. The egret eats flies that might hurt the rhino.

Boxer crabs can hold an anemone in each claw. They use the anemones to sting predators. An anemone is a sea animal.

✓ Lesson Checkpoint

1. How does a shark help a remora fish?

2. Math in Science Which is the best estimate of the weight of a rhinoceros: 35 pounds or 3,500 pounds?

Investigate How can you model a food web?

Many different living things make up a food web. All of the animals you see are part of a food web.

Materials

food web cards

tape

yarn

crayons or markers

What to Do

1 Choose a card. Tape it on your shirt. Stand in a circle with your group.

2 Look for living things that you eat or that eat you. Toss the ball of yarn to one of them.

3 Take turns until everyone is connected. Lay down the yarn and the cards.

 More Lab zone Activities **Take It to the Net** pearsonsuccessnet.com

4 Draw your food web and write the names of the living things.

My Food Web

Explain Your Results

1. **Infer** What do the web lines mean?
2. How did you **model** a real food web?

Begin to model the food web.

Go Further
How could you model a grassland food web? Make a plan and try it.

91

Measuring Length

hawk

These animals are from this chapter. They are some of the predators and prey in a grassland food web.

fox

raccoon

vole

Read the table. Find out how long some of the animals can grow to be.

Animal	Length in cm
Raccoon	100 cm
Vole	20 cm
Fox	80 cm
Hawk	60 cm

1. Which animal is the shortest?

2. Which animal is the longest?

3. How much longer is the fox than the vole?

4. Put the animals in order from shortest to longest.

Lab zone Take-Home Activity

Use a ruler. Find objects at home that match the length of each animal in the table. List the objects. Share your list with your family.

Vocabulary

Which picture goes with each word?

1. producer
2. consumer
3. food chain

What did you learn?

4. What do all animals need to live?

5. Name a predator from this chapter. What is its prey?

6. What are some ways animals help each other?

7. Infer What would happen to an ocean food web if there were no more kelp?

Cause and Effect

8. Read the captions.

It rained all day in this forest.

The mountain lion found shelter from the rain in a cave.

What **caused** the mountain lion to go into the cave?

Cause   Effect

Test Prep

Fill in the circle next to the correct answer.

9. Which animal finds shelter in an acacia plant?

  Ⓐ masked weaver

  Ⓑ egret

  Ⓒ cardinal fish

  Ⓓ ant

10. **Writing** in Science Describe a food chain from the chapter. Tell how energy passes through it.

Farmer

Read Together

Farmers have an important job! Some farmers work on farms that grow grains, fruits, and vegetables for food. Some farmers raise animals that give people milk, eggs, and meat.

When fruits and vegetables are ready, farmers pick them. They ship the fruits and vegetables off to factories or markets. Farmers milk cows. Farmers gather eggs from chickens. Many people depend on farmers for food.

Lab zone Take-Home Activity

Draw a picture of plants and animals on a farm. Tell how a farmer cares for the plants and animals in your picture.

You Will Discover

- ways that living things are like their parents.
- how plants and animals change as they grow.

Chapter 4

How Living Things Grow and Change

online
Student Edition
pearsonsuccessnet.com

How do living things grow in different ways?

life cycle

nymph

seed coat

98

Chapter 4
Vocabulary

life cycle   page 106

nymph   page 108

seed coat   page 114

germinate   page 114

seedling   page 114

germinate

Germinate means to begin to grow into a young plant.

seedling

Explore Which hand do different children use to write?

Materials

paper

crayon

scissors

tape

chart paper

What to Do

1 Trace the hand you use to write.

2 Write your name in the middle. Cut out the hand.

3 **Collect data** Tape your hand to the graph.

Be careful!

Scissors are sharp!

right hand

Tran

Michael

Emily

Juana

Anna

Gesgio

left hand

Explain Your Results

Infer What does the graph show?

How to Read Science

Reading Skills

TARGET SKILL
 Infer

Infer means to use what you know to answer a question.

Science Article

Carol is right-handed. She uses her right hand for writing and to drink from a glass. She uses both hands to button her coat. Ben is left-handed.

Apply It!

Infer Which hand do you think Ben would use to cut paper or throw a ball?

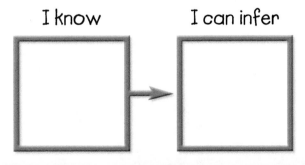

I know   I can infer

♪ Hi Little Turtle!

Sung to the tune of "Itsy Bitsy Spider"

Lyrics by Gerri Brioso & Richard Freitas/The Dovetail Group, Inc.

Look at the sea turtle coming from the sea.

Crawling on the sand, looking right at me.

Hey, little sea turtle, I would like to know,

How did you start out and how did you grow?

Science Songs ♪♫♪

How do sea turtles grow and change?

Living things need food and water. Living things grow and change. Living things can be parents. Plants and animals are living things.

The sea turtle is an animal. You will learn how a sea turtle grows and changes.

This toy turtle is a nonliving thing. It does not need food and water. It cannot grow and change. It cannot be a parent.

Sea Turtle Eggs

A sea turtle lives in the ocean. A sea turtle crawls onto a beach to lay eggs. A sea turtle uses its flippers to dig a hole in the sand. It lays eggs in the hole. Then the sea turtle covers the eggs with sand.

Sea turtles can lay many eggs at one time.

The eggs lay in the sand for about two months. Then the eggs are ready to hatch.

Baby turtles have a special tooth. The tooth helps them break open the egg's shell. Later, the tooth falls out.

A baby sea turtle hatches from its egg.

1. ✔ Checkpoint   How do baby sea turtles get out of the egg?

2. Math in Science   Suppose 3 sea turtles each laid 100 eggs. How many eggs were laid all together?

The Life Cycle of a Sea Turtle

The way a living thing grows and changes is called its **life cycle.** Follow the arrows to see the life cycle of a sea turtle.

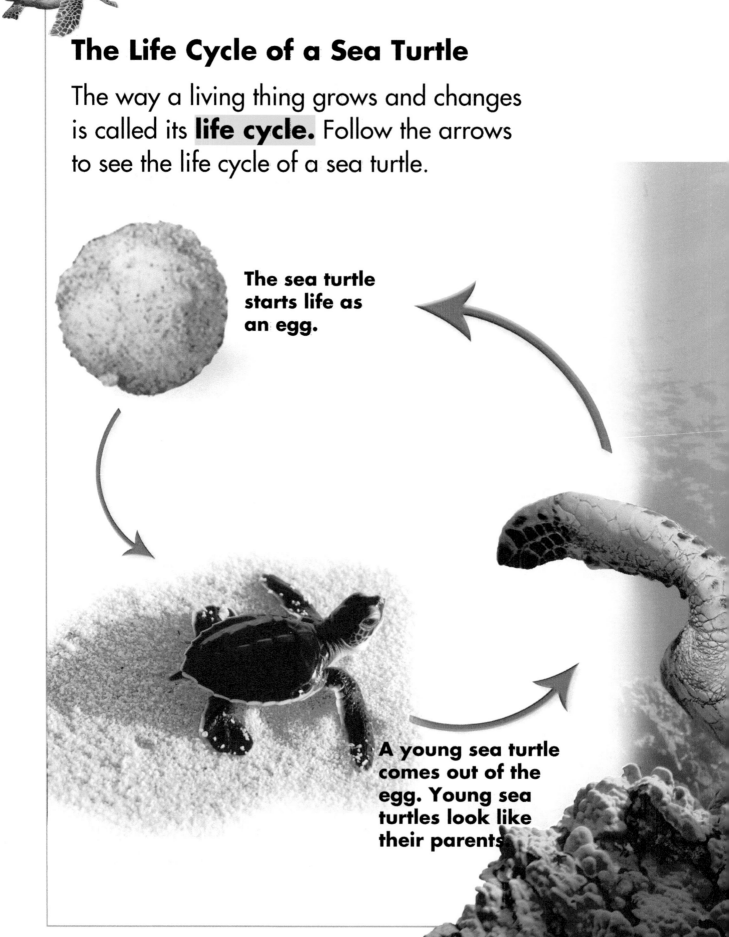

The sea turtle starts life as an egg.

A young sea turtle comes out of the egg. Young sea turtles look like their parents.

1. How do sea turtles start life?

2. **Social Studies** in Science Look at a map of the United States. Find some places where sea turtles might lay eggs.

One day, the sea turtle may have young of its own. A new life cycle begins.

What is the life cycle of a dragonfly?

The life cycles of insects are different from the life cycles of other animals. Many young insects are called **nymphs.** Nymphs look a lot like their parents, but their wings are still growing. Nymphs shed their outside covering many times as they grow.

Dragonflies often lay eggs in the water.

A nymph hatches from the dragonfly egg. First, the nymph lives in the water. Then, the nymph crawls to the land.

The nymph has shed its covering one last time. Now it is an adult dragonfly with wings to fly. It may lay eggs.

☑ Lesson Checkpoint

1. Tell the stages of a dragonfly life cycle in order.

2. 🔁 **Infer** Why doesn't a nymph need wings?

Lesson 3

What is the life cycle of a horse?

A horse is a mammal. Most young mammals grow inside their mothers. Young mammals drink milk from their mother.

A young horse is called a foal.

The foal grows and grows. It looks like its parents.

110

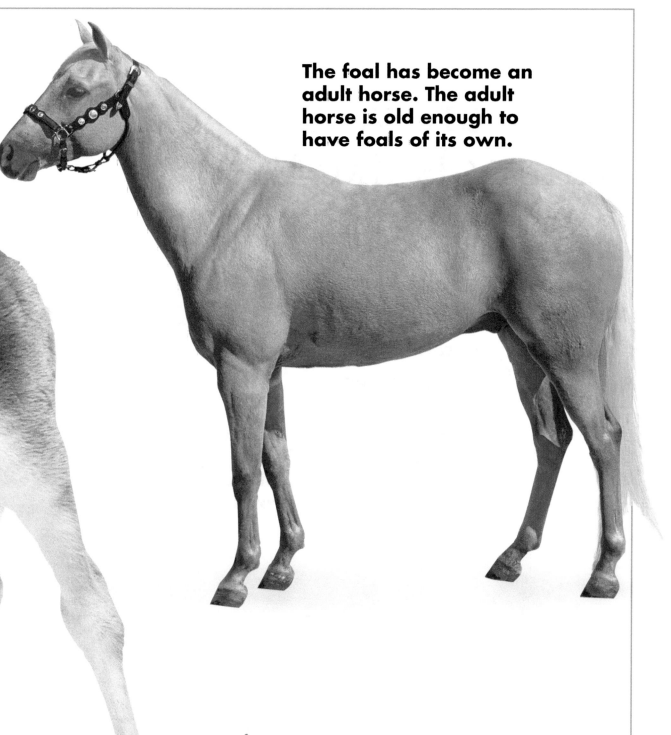

The foal has become an adult horse. The adult horse is old enough to have foals of its own.

✔ Lesson Checkpoint

1. **Infer** What is food for a foal?

2. **Writing** in Science Tell what you know about the life cycle of a horse.

How are young animals like their parents?

Young animals often look like their parents in shape and color. Yet some young animals look different from their parents.

Young penguins are covered with fuzzy down feathers. The feathers become white and black as the penguin grows.

These kittens all have the same parents. Yet they look different from each other.

Giraffes have brown spots. Each giraffe has its own pattern of spots. No two patterns are the same.

The spots on the adult giraffe are darker than the spots on its young.

✔ Lesson Checkpoint

1. How are young penguins different from their parents?

2. **Writing** in Science Tell how you think the kittens are like their parents.

Lesson 5

What is the life cycle of a bean plant?

Most plants grow from seeds. A seed has a hard outer covering called a **seed coat.** A seed coat protects the seed.

Each seed contains a tiny plant and stored food. The tiny plant uses the stored food as it grows. A seed that gets enough water and air may **germinate,** or begin to grow. Roots from the germinated seed grow down into the ground. A stem grows up. A seedling grows out of the ground. A **seedling** is a young plant.

Seeds are the beginning of a bean plant life cycle.

The bean seed germinates and starts to grow.

A seedling grows from the seed.

Seed coat

SciLinks Take It to the Net
pearsonsuccessnet.com   keyword: seedling
code: g2p114

The plant continues to grow. The flowers on an adult plant make seeds. Some seeds from an adult plant will grow into new plants.

The plant continues to grow and change. It becomes an adult.

√ Lesson Checkpoint

1. How does a seed coat help a seed?

2. **Math** in Science A farmer plants 5 rows of bean plants. There are 10 bean plants in each row. How many bean plants did the farmer plant in all? Skip count to find the answer.

How are young plants like their parents?

Young plants are usually like the parent plant in color and shape. Young plants can be different from the parent plant in some ways too.

A young saguaro cactus has the same shape as an adult. It has the same color as an adult.

An adult saguaro cactus has arms.

A young saguaro cactus does not have arms.

116

These flowers are called foxgloves. Foxgloves grow leaves during their first year of life. They grow flowers during their second year of life. Look at the picture. The foxglove flowers all have the same shape. The foxglove flowers have different colors.

✓ **Lesson Checkpoint**

1. How are the foxgloves alike and different?

2. **Art** in Science Draw a young saguaro cactus and an old saguaro cactus. Write how they are different.

How do people grow and change?

People are alike in some ways. All people change as they grow. You used to be a baby. You are a child now. You have lost some of your first teeth. You have grown taller. What are some other ways you have changed?

This boy has changed since he was a baby. Now he can read and talk.

You will keep changing as you get older. You will get taller. You will become a teenager. Later, you will become an adult. Adults keep changing too. Adults do not grow taller. An adult's skin will begin to wrinkle. The color of an adult's hair may change to gray or white.

The members of this family will keep changing.

1. ✓ Checkpoint   What is one way all people are alike?

2. What are some ways people grow and change?

How People Are Different

People are different in some ways too.
Some people are short. Some people
are tall. Some people have brown eyes.
Some people have blue eyes. People have
different hair colors. People have different
skin colors.

**Look at the many
ways these children
are different.**

Children in the same family might look like each other. They might look different from each other too. How might children in the same family look alike? How might they look different?

Parents and their children may look alike in some ways. They may look different in other ways. Look at the family in the picture on this page. How are the children like their parents? How are they different?

People in a family do not look exactly alike.

✓ Lesson Checkpoint

1. What are some ways people can be different from each other?

2. **Infer** Where did the children in the picture get their dark eyes?

Guided Inquiry

Investigate How does a caterpillar grow and change?

Living things change as they grow. Some insects look different from their parents.

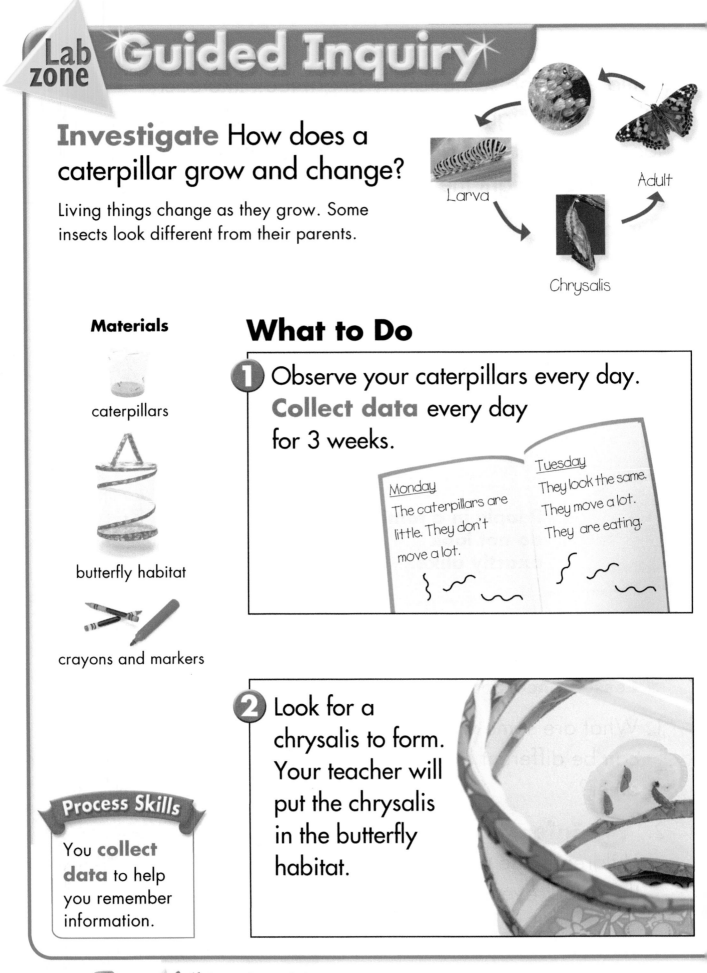

Larva

Chrysalis

Adult

Materials

caterpillars

butterfly habitat

crayons and markers

What to Do

1 Observe your caterpillars every day. **Collect data** every day for 3 weeks.

Monday
The caterpillars are little. They don't move a lot.

Tuesday
They look the same.
They move a lot.
They are eating.

Process Skills

You **collect data** to help you remember information.

2 Look for a chrysalis to form. Your teacher will put the chrysalis in the butterfly habitat.

3 Continue to collect data. **Predict** what will happen next.

They're alive! Handle with care.

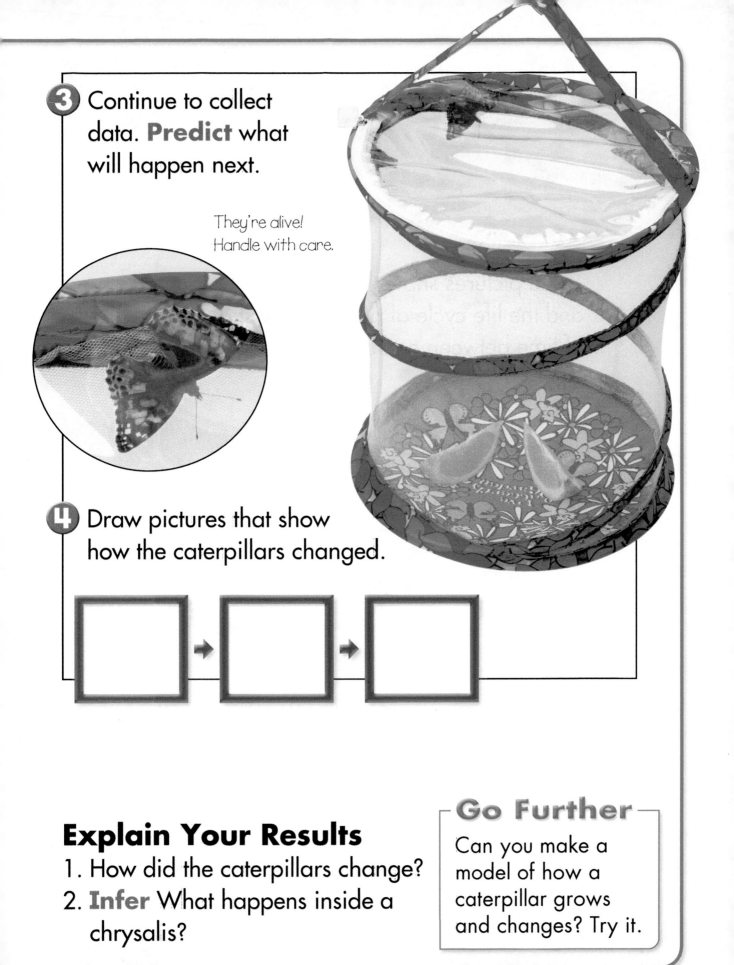

4 Draw pictures that show how the caterpillars changed.

Explain Your Results
1. How did the caterpillars change?
2. **Infer** What happens inside a chrysalis?

Go Further

Can you make a model of how a caterpillar grows and changes? Try it.

Measuring Time

These pictures show the life cycle of a butterfly and the life cycle of a frog. They show the amount of time between each step in the life cycles.

A butterfly life cycle

4. butterfly

1. egg

14 days

4 days

3. pupa

2. caterpillar

12 days

@ Tools Take It to the Net
pearsonsuccessnet.com

1. How many days does it take a butterfly egg to hatch into a caterpillar?

2. How many days does it take for a butterfly egg to become a butterfly? Write a number sentence.

It takes 2 weeks for frog eggs to hatch into tadpoles. How many days is this? Write a number sentence.

A frog life cycle

1. egg

2 weeks

3. frog

16 weeks

2. tadpole

Lab zone Take-Home Activity

A caterpillar grows to be about 5 centimeters long. What other things might be 5 centimeters long? Measure to find out.

Vocabulary

Which picture goes with each word?

1. seed coat
2. life cycle
3. nymph
4. seedling

What did you learn?

5. How are people alike and different?

6. Compare the life cycles of a dragonfly and a horse. How are they alike and different?

7. What does germinate mean?

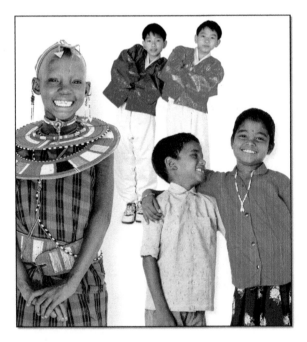

8. **Infer** Why does a baby turtle's special tooth fall out after it hatches from the egg?

Infer

9. People are wearing heavy coats and hats outside. They are wearing gloves and scarves. What can you **infer** about the weather?

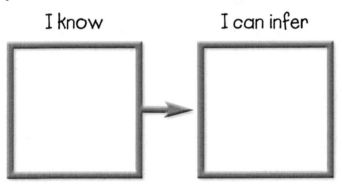

I know → I can infer

Test Prep

Fill in the circle next to the correct answer.

10. What kind of animal changes from an egg to a nymph?
    Ⓐ mammal
    Ⓑ insect
    Ⓒ reptile
    Ⓓ bird

11. **Writing** in Science How might living things be like their parents? Make a list.

SAVE the Sea Turtles

Meet Mario J. Mota

Dr. Mota

Read Together

Dr. Mario Mota is a marine biologist. He works at NASA. Dr. Mota studies turtle biology. He uses some of the tools used on the space shuttle to study the turtles.

Dr. Mota was born in Africa. When Dr. Mota was young, he liked to fish. Dr. Mota always loved the ocean. He knew he wanted to work by the ocean.

Sea turtles lay their eggs on or near the same beach where they hatched. They lay more than 100 eggs in each nest!

Lab zone Take-Home Activity

Baby sea turtles hatch from eggs. Work with your family. Make a list of other animals that hatch from eggs.

Test-Taking Strategies

▷ Find Important Words
Choose the Right Answer
Use Information from Text and Graphics
Write Your Answer

Find Important Words

There are important words in science questions. These words help you understand the questions.

Megan lives near a big pond where lots of frogs live. One day, Megan sat on the grass by the pond. She liked watching the frogs. Megan saw one frog sitting very still. The frog's tongue zipped out. It caught a tasty insect to eat.

Read the question.

What is one thing that frogs eat?

Ⓐ ponds
Ⓑ sandwiches
Ⓒ grass
Ⓓ insects

First, find important words in the question. The most important words are **frogs** and **eat.** Next, find important words in the text that match the important words in the question. Use the words to answer the question.

Unit A Wrap-Up

Chapter 1

How do plants live in their habitats?

- Plants have adaptations that help them live in different environments.

Chapter 2

How are animals different from each other?

- Animals can be put into two groups. One group of animals has backbones. The other group of animals does not have backbones.

Chapter 3

How do living things help each other?

- Living things help each other in different ways. Animals and plants that need each other for food are part of a food chain.

Chapter 4

How do living things grow in different ways?

- Living things have different life cycles. A life cycle is the way a living thing grows and changes. Plants and animals have life cycles.

Performance Assessment

How Can You Sort Animals?

- Cut out pictures of different animals that live on the land, in water, and in the air.

- Put the animals into groups.

- Tell which animals have backbones and which animals do not have backbones.

Read More About Life Science!

Look for books like these in your library.

heron   cardinal

Experiment Which bird beak can crush seeds?

Look at the heron's beak. Look at the cardinal's beak. How are the beaks alike? How are they different?

Materials

2 clothespins

2 craft sticks

glue

straw pieces

Ask a question.
Which bird uses its beak to crush seeds? **Use models** to learn more.

Make a hypothesis.
Which crushes better, a model of a heron's beak, or a model of a cardinal's beak? Tell what you think.

Plan a fair test.
Be sure to use the same kind of clothespins.

Do your test.

1 Make a model of a heron's beak. Glue 2 craft sticks to a clothespin. Let the glue dry. Use the other clothespin as a model of a cardinal's beak. Use a piece of straw as a model of a seed.

2 Use the heron's beak.
Pick up a seed. Try it again.

3 Use the cardinal's beak.
Pick up a seed. Try it again.

models of seeds

model of a
heron's beak

model of a
cardinal's beak

4 **Observe.** Which beak crushes the seeds?

Collect and record data.

	Did the beak crush the seed? (Circle one for each beak.)
Heron's beak	
Cardinal's beak	

Tell your conclusion.
Which model crushes a straw?
Infer Which bird uses its beak to crush seeds?

Go Further
Which beak will pick up seeds faster? Try it and find out.

End with a Poem

THE SEA TURTLE

The sea turtle spends her life in the sea,
It's a wonderful place for her to be.
She dives and she grabs
Shrimp, jellyfish, and crabs,
She gets all of her food for free.

The sea turtle scrambles onto the shore,
Ready to lay ninety-five eggs or more.
Then she creeps in slow motion
Back down to the ocean,
Leaving babies behind to explore.

Science Fair Projects

Full Inquiry

Using Scientific Methods
1. Ask a question.
2. Make a hypothesis.
3. Plan a fair test.
4. Do your test.
5. Collect and record data.
6. Tell your conclusion.
7. Go further.

Idea 1
Temperature and Seeds

Plan a project. Find out if seeds will grow faster in a warm place or a cold place.

Idea 2
Jumping Insects

Plan a project. Find out if crickets or grasshoppers are better jumpers.

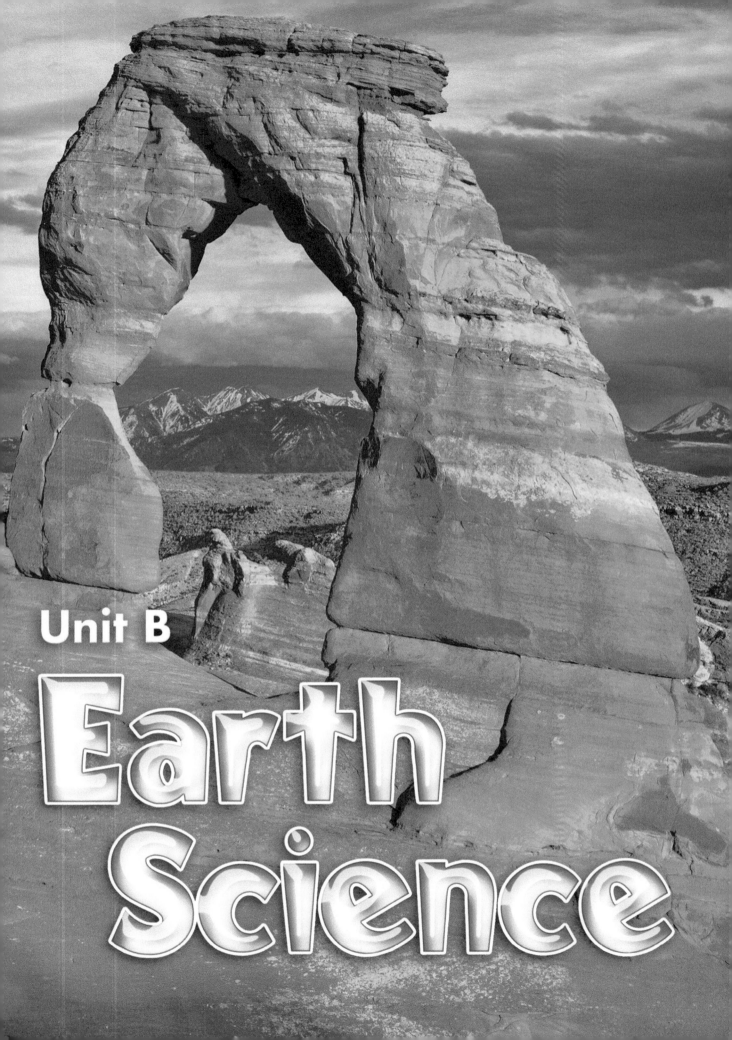

Unit B

Earth Science

Unit B

Chapter 5 Earth's Land, Air, and Water

Directed Inquiry   How are soils different?

Guided Inquiry   How do worms change the soil?

Activity Flip Chart   How does erosion affect land?
How can you reuse something?

Quick Activity
Transparencies   What are some natural resources?
What are rocks and soil like?
How are plants used by people?
How does water change rocks?
How can you help Earth?

Chapter 6 Earth's Weather and Seasons

Directed Inquiry   How much rain falls?

Guided Inquiry   How can you measure weather changes?

Activity Flip Chart   What happens when cold air meets warm air?
How can you tell that water is moving?

Quick Activity
Transparencies   What are some kinds of weather?
Where does water go?
What do you like about spring?
What do you like about summer?
What do you like about fall?
What do you like about winter?
What are thunderstorms like?

Chapter 7 Fossils and Dinosaurs

Directed Inquiry   Which fossils match the plants and animals?

Guided Inquiry   How can you make a model of a fossil?

Activity Flip Chart   How do paleontologists dig for fossils?
How can you tell what made the tracks?

Quick Activity
Transparencies   What are fossils?
How can fossils teach us about the past?
What were dinosaurs like?
How does an eggshell help baby chickens?

Unit B

Full Inquiry   Does gravel, sand, or soil make the best imprint?

STEM Project   Compost Gold

You Will Discover

how people use Earth's natural resources.

ways that people can take care of Earth's natural resources.

Chapter 5

Earth's Land, Air, and Water

Web Games
Take It to the Net
pearsonsuccessnet.com

online
Student Edition
pearsonsuccessnet.com

What are Earth's natural resources?

weathering

natural resource

san

minerals

erosion

138

Chapter 5 Vocabulary

natural resource
page 143

boulder page 146

sand page 146

minerals page 147

erosion page 152

weathering
page 153

pollution page 154

recycle page 157

boulder

pollution

recycle

Explore How are soils different?

Materials

plates with soils

hand lens

dropper

cup with water

What to Do

1 Observe the soils. Look, smell, and touch.

2 Use the hand lens. Observe the smallest bits of soil.

3 Add water. Observe how the soils soak up the water.

Label the plates.

sandy soil

potting soil

Process Skills

You **observe** when you look, smell, and touch.

Explain Your Results

Observe How are the soils alike? How are they different?

Reading Skills

TARGET SKILL

Picture Clues

Pictures can give you clues about what you read.

Science Article

Soil

There are many kinds of living things in soil. Plants live in soil. Worms and other animals live in soil too.

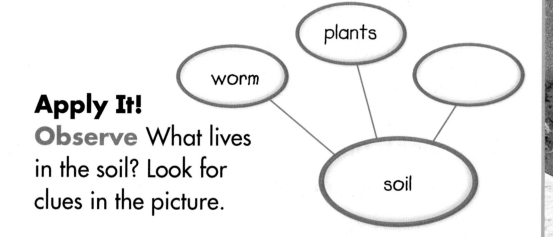

Apply It!
Observe What lives in the soil? Look for clues in the picture.

♪ Natural Resources

Sung to the tune of "Did You Ever See a Lassie?"
Lyrics by Gerri Brioso & Richard Freitas/The Dovetail Group, Inc.

Earth has many natural resources,

Resources, resources.

Name some natural resources,

We need and use.

Sunlight, and water and air are all resources.

Natural resources,

We need and use.

What are natural resources?

Sunlight, water, and forests are natural resources. A **natural resource** is a useful thing that comes from nature. Oil and coal are natural resources too.

Some natural resources cannot be replaced after they are used up. Oil and coal cannot be replaced.

Some natural resources can be replaced after they are used. New trees can be planted to replace trees that are cut down for wood.

Some natural resources can never be used up. Sunlight, water, and air will never be used up.

Water and Air

Water is a natural resource. Plants, animals, and people need water to live. Ponds, rivers, streams, and lakes have fresh water. Oceans have salt water.

People use water in many ways. People drink water. People use water to cook and clean.

Air is a natural resource. Plants, animals, and people need air to live. Air is all around us. Wind is moving air.

✓ Lesson Checkpoint

1. Name some natural resources.

2. **Writing** in Science Make a list. What are some ways you use water every day?

Plants need water to live.

Air is used to fill this soccer ball.

This fishing boat brings fish from the ocean for people to eat.

Hot air fills this balloon.

What are rocks and soil like?

Rocks are natural resources. Rocks come in many shapes, colors, and sizes. A very big rock is called a **boulder.** People use rocks to build houses.

Wind, rain, and ice can break rocks into smaller pieces. **Sand** is made of tiny pieces of rock. Some rocks can be smaller than grains of sand. People use sand to build roads.

Minerals are a natural resource. **Minerals** are nonliving materials that come from Earth. Rocks are made of minerals. Gold, iron, and silver are minerals.

Quartz is a mineral used to make glass.

Copper is a mineral. Some pots are made from copper.

1. ✓Checkpoint Name four minerals.

2. Math in Science Think about a boulder. Is the length of a boulder closer to 10 inches or 10 feet? Explain your answer.

Soil

Soil is a natural resource. Soil covers most of Earth's land. Many soils are a mixture of clay, sand, and humus. Soil contains air and water. Most plants grow in soil.

Soil can be different colors. Soil can be hard or soft. Soil can feel wet or dry.

Sandy soil is loose. It feels dry and rough.

Clay soil has very small pieces. Clay soil feels smooth. It feels soft and sticky.

Humus is a part of soil that comes from living things.

Different kinds of plants grow best in different kinds of soil. Plants may grow well in one kind of soil. They may not grow as well in another kind of soil.

✓ **Lesson Checkpoint**

1. Describe sandy soil, clay soil, and humus.

2. 🎯 Use **picture clues.** Tell how sandy soil, clay soil, and humus are different.

How do people use plants?

Plants are a natural resource. People use plants in many ways. Plants can be used to make food, shelter, and clothing. The pictures show some things you use every day that are made from plants.

People use cotton to make clothes. This T-shirt is made from cotton.

People use wood from pine trees to build houses.

1. What is one way that people use cotton plants?

2. 🎯 Use **picture clues.** What things are made from trees?

People use wheat to make food. This bread is made from wheat.

People use trees to make paper. What are some ways people use paper?

How does Earth change?

Earth is always changing. Erosion can change Earth. **Erosion** happens when rocks or soil are moved by water or wind.

Plants can help prevent erosion. The roots on plants hold the soil in place.

Look at what erosion can do to a field!

Weathering can change Earth too.
Weathering is the breaking apart
and changing of rocks. Water can cause
weathering. Changes in temperature can
cause weathering.

✓ Lesson Checkpoint

1. How does weathering change Earth?

2. **Writing** in Science   Look for erosion
near where you live. Write about
what you see.

**Animals that dig homes
in soil can change Earth
too. Gophers change the
shape of the land.**

How can people help protect Earth?

People change the Earth by causing pollution. **Pollution** happens when something harmful is added to the land, air, or water. Pollution can cause some plants and animals to get sick or die.

Many people have started working together to help reduce pollution. They want to make sure plants and animals stay safe. They want to take care of the Earth.

This lake was once polluted.

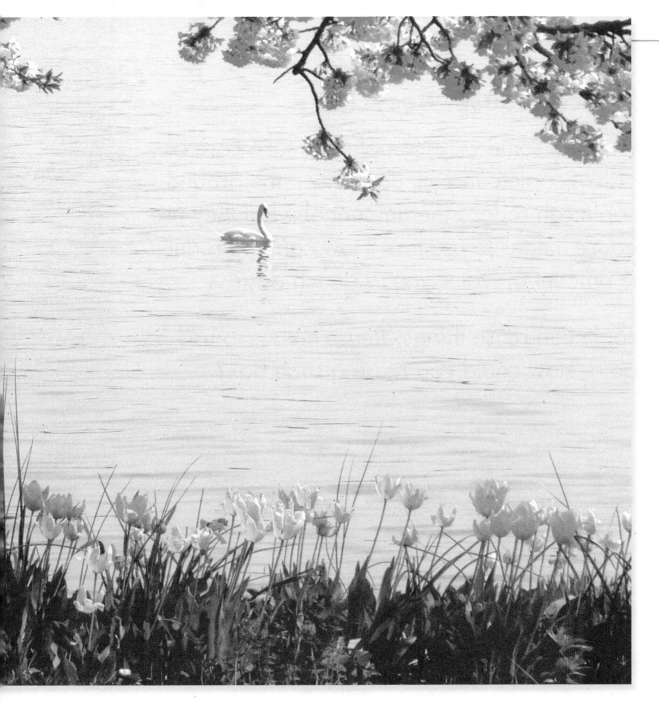

People worked to clean up this lake. It is now safe for plants and animals.

1. ✔ Checkpoint What is pollution?

2. Health in Science What are some ways clean water is important to people?

Reduce, Reuse, Recycle

What are some ways people can take care of Earth? People can pick up litter on the ground. People can reduce the amount of what they use. *Reduce* means to use less. How can you reduce the amount of water you use each day?

People can reuse things. *Reuse* means to use again. How could you reuse a shoe box?

Plastic milk cartons can be recycled to make new objects.

People can recycle. **Recycle** means to change something so it can be used again. Cans, glass, paper, plastic, and metal can all be recycled. Some parts of this playground were made from recycled plastic milk bottles!

1. ✓**Checkpoint** What can you do to help take care of Earth?

2. **Art** in Science Collect empty containers and other trash. Use them to make art.

Protecting Plants and Animals

Chop! People cut down trees. Some animals live in trees. People plant new trees. Animals can make their homes in the new trees.

Campfires can turn into forest fires. Always put out campfires.

Wind and fire can kill trees. New trees start to grow back after a forest fire. These new trees might grow big and tall.

People build homes and factories on land. Plants and animals that lived on the land may have no place to go. People take plants and animals to a refuge. A refuge is a safe place to live. People cannot build on a refuge.

This bird lives in a refuge in Florida. People can see plants and animals at the refuge.

✔ Lesson Checkpoint

1. What are some ways people can help protect plants and animals?

2. **Technology** in Science
   Read an article about wildfires on the Internet.

Investigate How do worms change the soil?

Compost is a mixture of soil with other things like leaves and grass. How will worms change compost?

Materials

plastic gloves

bags with soil

leaves

worms

Filling in a chart can help you **collect data**.

What to Do

1 Wear gloves. Put leaves in both bags.

2 Put worms in one bag.

Be sure to close the bags.

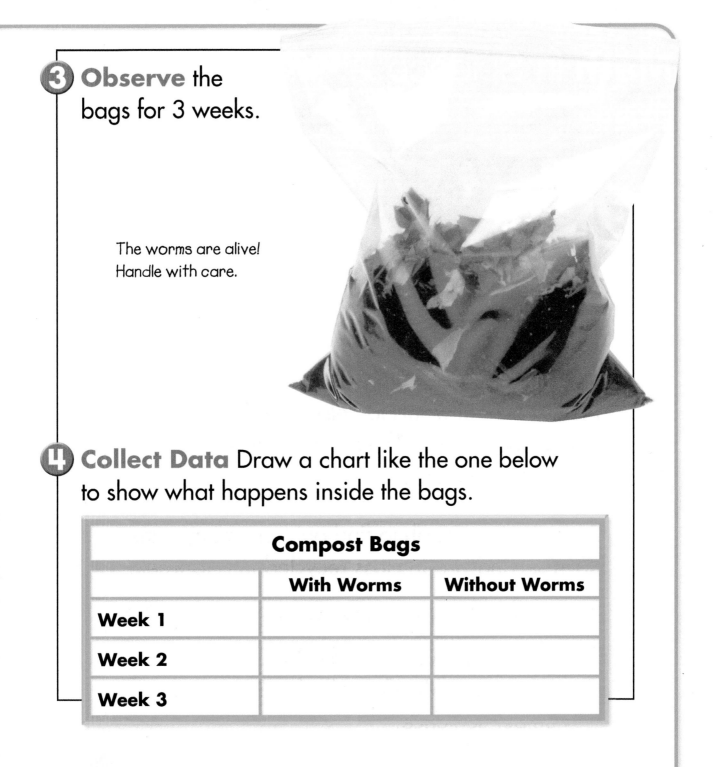

3 **Observe** the bags for 3 weeks.

The worms are alive! Handle with care.

4 **Collect Data** Draw a chart like the one below to show what happens inside the bags.

Compost Bags		
	With Worms	**Without Worms**
Week 1		
Week 2		
Week 3		

Explain Your Results

1. Which bag had more leaves after 3 weeks?
2. **Infer** What happened to the leaves?

Go Further

What will happen if you use more worms? Investigate to find out.

Recycling Bar Graph

Nelson School wants to help keep the environment clean. The second graders decided to recycle cans.

Read the bar graph to find out how many cans each second-grade class recycled in one week.

1. How many cans did Mr. Green's class recycle?

2. How many more cans did Mrs. Hill's class recycle than Mr. Green's class? Write a number sentence.

e Tools Take It to the Net
pearsonsuccessnet.com

Number of Cans That We Recycled

	10	20	30	40	50
Mr. Green					
Mrs. Hill					
Mrs. Lee					

Lab zone Take-Home Activity

Make a list of the different things that you and your family recycle.

Vocabulary

Which picture goes with each word?

1. boulder
2. mineral
3. erosion
4. sand
5. recycle
6. pollution

What did you learn?

7. Name some of Earth's natural resources.

8. How does erosion change Earth?

9. **Observe** Look at a plant outside. Describe the soil.

Picture Clues

10. **Use picture clues** Tell how people use air.

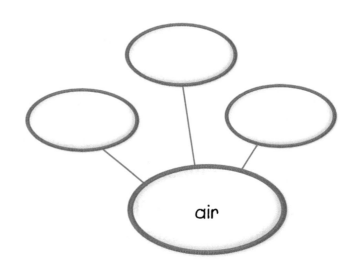

Test Prep

Fill in the circle next to the correct answer.

11. What do people make from cotton?

Ⓐ furniture
Ⓑ maple syrup
Ⓒ clothes
Ⓓ playgrounds

12. Writing in Science List some things people throw away. Tell how you could reuse one of those things.

Looking out for Earth

Many satellites move around Earth. NASA scientists send satellites to space. Scientists use satellites to take pictures of Earth's natural resources. Satellite pictures can show dirty air over cities. The satellite pictures can also show how well crops are growing. Spotting forest fires is easier from satellites too.

The smoky area shows a forest fire.

A satellite takes pictures of new plants.

NASA satellites take pictures of Earth. Draw a picture of what you think Earth looks like from space.

Forester

Read Together

Foresters have many jobs. They build roads in forests. They work to prevent forest fires. They decide how many trees can be cut. They plant new trees.

Foresters study forests and learn how to keep them healthy. They help protect plants and animals that live in forests. Foresters teach other people how to be safe in the forest.

Lab zone Take-Home Activity

Tell what job you would like to do if you were a forester. Tell your family about how your job would help the forest.

You Will Discover

- that there are patterns in the weather.
- how weather changes from season to season.

Chapter 6
Earth's Weather and Seasons

online
Student Edition
pearsonsuccessnet.com

How does weather change?

tornado

water cycle

evaporate   condense

Chapter 6 Vocabulary

water cycle page 178

evaporate page 179

condense page 179

migrate page 184

hibernate page 186

lightning page 188

tornado page 190

hurricane page 192

hurricane

lightning

migrate

hibernate

Explore How much rain falls?

Make a tool to measure how much rain falls.

Materials

jar

tape

ruler

black pencil

What to Do

1 Number each centimeter line up to 12. Start at the bottom of the tape.

2 Fasten tape to the jar.

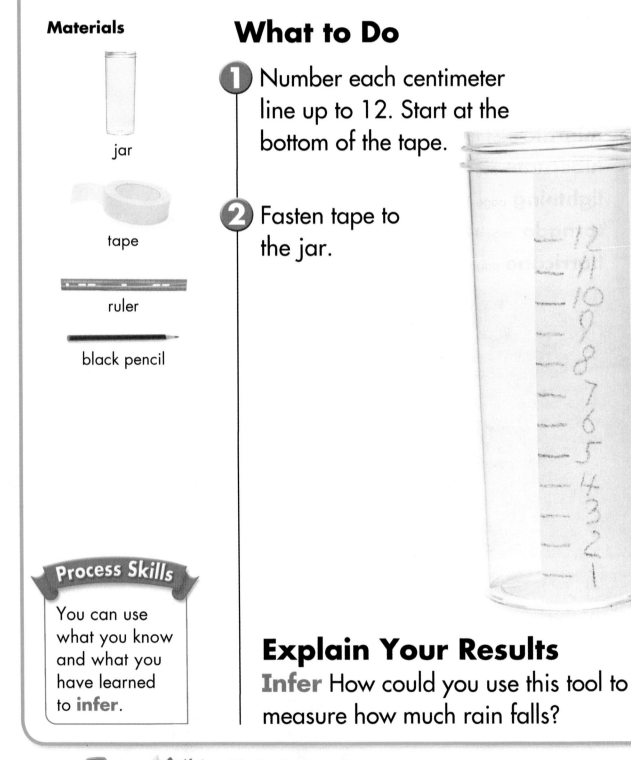

Explain Your Results

Infer How could you use this tool to measure how much rain falls?

How to Read Science

Reading Skills

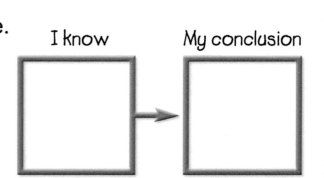

TARGET SKILL
Draw Conclusions

You draw conclusions when you decide about something you see or read.

Science Picture

Apply It!
Look at the picture.
Infer What is the weather like outside?

I know		My conclusion
	→	

♪ What's the Weather?

Sung to the tune of "Yankee Doodle"
Lyrics by Gerri Brioso & Richard Freitas/The Dovetail Group, Inc.

There's all kinds of weather and
Of that I'm really sure.
Just open up a window
Or peek out an open door.

What are some kinds of weather?

You wake up in the morning. How do you know what to wear? Check the weather!

Weather is what the air outside is like. Temperature tells you how hot or cold something is. Look for any clouds. If tree branches are moving, the wind is blowing.

A windy day is perfect for flying a kite!

Heavy rains can fall in spring and summer.

Some places get snow in winter.

Hail is pieces of ice that fall from clouds.

Wet and Dry Weather

Clouds can help tell you what kind of weather is coming. Clouds are made up of drops of water and small pieces of ice. When the small pieces of ice join together, they start to fall.

Snowflakes fall in cold weather. Blizzards are snow storms with strong winds. In warm air, snow melts into rain as it falls. Sleet is rain that freezes as it falls. Snow, rain, and sleet are different kinds of wet weather.

The land is very dry in a drought.

A drought can happen when it does not rain for a long time. A drought is one kind of dry weather. There may not be enough water for many plants and animals during a drought.

Some plants may not be able to live in a drought.

✓ Lesson Checkpoint

1. What are three kinds of wet weather?

2. **Technology** in Science Go to www.nws.noaa.gov on the Internet. What will the weather be like tomorrow where you live?

Lesson 2

What is the water cycle?

The way water moves from the clouds to Earth and back to the clouds again is called the **water cycle.** Look at this picture. Follow the steps in the water cycle.

Water falls from the clouds. The water might be in the form of rain, snow, hail, or sleet.

Water flows into rivers, lakes, and oceans.

 SciLinks Take It to the Net pearsonsuccessnet.com | keyword: water cycle code: g2p178

When the water vapor in clouds gets cold, it condenses. **Condense** means to change into tiny drops of water. The tiny drops of water form clouds.

Energy from the Sun makes some of the water evaporate. Water **evaporates** when it changes into water vapor. *Water vapor* is water in the air. You cannot see water vapor.

✓ Lesson Checkpoint

1. What are the steps in the water cycle?

2. ↻ **Draw Conclusions** How does energy from the Sun change water in water puddles?

What is spring?

Weather in many places changes with the seasons. The four seasons are spring, summer, fall, and winter. The seasons repeat every year.

Some spring days are cool. Other spring days are warm. Spring days can be rainy. The rain helps plants grow. Many animals have babies in the spring.

✓ Lesson Checkpoint

1. Tell about two things that can happen in spring.

2. Writing in Science
   Write two sentences. What are some things you like to do in spring?

This mother deer had her baby in the spring.

180

Holland, Michigan

Holland, Michigan is known for its beautiful tulips. Tulips bloom in the spring.

Spring can be very rainy.

New leaves start growing on trees in the spring.

What is summer?

Summer comes after spring. Summer has more daylight hours than spring. Summer often has hot days and warm nights. In most places, summer is the hottest season of the year. Green leaves grow on many trees and other plants. Flowers, fruits, and vegetables grow.

✓ **Lesson Checkpoint**

1. How are daylight hours in spring and summer different?

2. **Art** in Science Draw a picture of your neighborhood in summer.

You can see many animal families in the summer.

Charleston,
South Carolina

Parks can be
beautiful in
the summer.
This park is in
Charleston, South
Carolina.

Many people
like to grow
vegetables in
the summer.

The adult duck is
swimming with
her babies on a
summer day.

What is fall?

Fall comes after summer. There are fewer hours of daylight in fall than in summer. The air begins to get cooler.

The leaves on some trees turn different colors in fall. Then the leaves fall to the ground.

Some animals, such as chipmunks and squirrels, begin to store food for the winter. Other animals **migrate,** or move to a different place.

✓ **Lesson Checkpoint**

1. What are two things animals might do in fall?

2. 🎯 **Draw Conclusions** Suppose you see many groups of geese flying south in the fall. What do you think is happening?

In fall, some animals gather food for the winter.

Bloomington, Indiana

Look at the trees in Bloomington, Indiana. The leaves have turned different colors.

Sandhill cranes migrate every fall.

In fall, farmers harvest crops.

What is winter?

Winter comes after fall. In some places, winter can be very cold. It may even snow. Ponds and streams may turn to ice.

Winter has fewer daylight hours than fall. Many trees have no leaves.

Some animals hibernate in winter. **Hibernate** means to have a long, deep sleep. Animals that hibernate come out in spring to look for food.

✓ **Lesson Checkpoint**

1. What happens when an animal hibernates?

2. **Writing** in Science Write in your journal about winter where you live. What is the weather like?

Most bears hibernate in winter.

Adirondack,
New York

There can
be heavy
snowstorms in
Adirondack,
New York.

You can see
many trees and
roofs covered
with snow in
winter.

It is fun to play in
the snow. Be sure
to wear coats
and hats.

187

What are some kinds of bad weather?

A thunderstorm is a kind of bad weather. A thunderstorm has heavy rain with thunder and lightning. **Lightning** is a flash of light in the sky. Thunder is the loud sound that you hear after lightning flashes. Sometimes thunderstorms have hail and strong winds.

1. ✔ Checkpoint What is lightning?
2. Art in Science Make a safety poster. Show how to stay safe during a thunderstorm.

A lot of rain can fall during a thunderstorm.

Thunderstorm Safety

- Find shelter in a building or car.

- Stay away from water.

- Stay away from metal objects.

- Do not stand under a tree.

- Do not use telephones.

- Keep away from objects that use electricity.

Tornadoes

Tornadoes can happen during thunderstorms. A **tornado** has very strong winds that come down from clouds in the shape of a funnel.

Tornadoes form quickly. It is hard to predict when a tornado will happen. A tornado that touches the ground can destroy things.

Tornadoes can happen in spring or summer.

1. ✓ Checkpoint What is one way to stay safe during a tornado?

2. Writing in Science Tell what a tornado is like.

Tornado Safety

- **Go to the basement or an inside hall, closet, or bathroom.**

- **Sit under the stairs or near an inner wall.**

- **Keep away from windows, water, metal, and objects that use electricity.**

- **Cover your head.**

- **If you cannot get to shelter, lie flat in a low place.**

Hurricanes

A **hurricane** is a large storm
that starts over warm ocean water.
A hurricane has heavy rains.
The rains can cause floods.

A hurricane has very strong winds.
The winds can knock down trees
and buildings.

√ **Lesson Checkpoint**

1. What is a hurricane?

2. **Draw Conclusions** What
might happen to objects left
outside during a hurricane?

192

Hurricane Safety

- Move away from the ocean if you can.

- Board up windows.

- Bring loose objects inside.

- Keep extra water on hand for drinking.

- Check the batteries in your flashlights and radio.

- During the storm, stay inside. Stay away from windows.

This picture shows the eye of a hurricane. The eye is a calm area in the center of the storm.

Lab zone Guided Inquiry

Investigate How can you measure weather changes?

There are many tools for measuring weather. A rain gauge measures rainfall. A thermometer measures temperature.

Materials

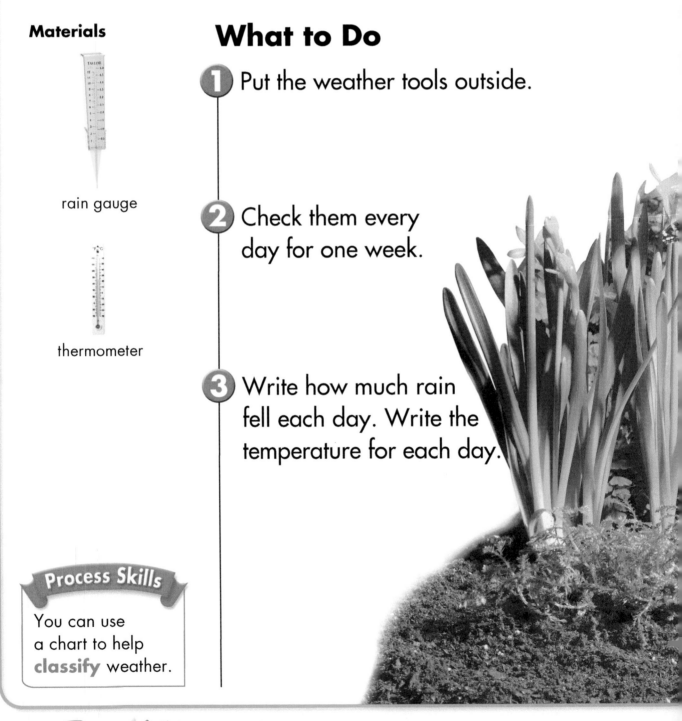

rain gauge

thermometer

What to Do

1 Put the weather tools outside.

2 Check them every day for one week.

3 Write how much rain fell each day. Write the temperature for each day.

Process Skills

You can use a chart to help **classify** weather.

Temperature and Rain for One Week

Day of the Week	rain gauge	thermometer
Monday		
Tuesday		
Wednesday		
Thursday		
Friday		

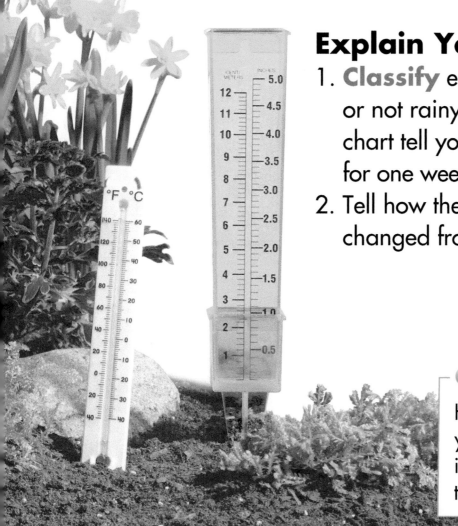

Explain Your Results

1. **Classify** each day as rainy or not rainy. What does your chart tell you about the weather for one week?
2. Tell how the weather changed from day to day.

Go Further

How much rain do you think might fall in 5 days? Measure to find out.

Charting Favorite Seasons

Nan wanted to find out what her classmates' favorite seasons were. She made a chart to show this information.

ⓔ **Tools** Take It to the Net
pearsonsuccessnet.com

Look at the chart. Answer the questions.

Spring   ☺ ☺ ☺

Summer   ☺ ☺ ☺ ☺ ☺ ☺ ☺ ☺ ☺

Fall   ☺ ☺ ☺ ☺ ☺

Winter   ☺ ☺ ☺ ☺ ☺ ☺ ☺ ☺

1. How many children liked summer best?

2. Use <, >, or =. Compare how many children liked summer best to how many liked winter best.

3. How many more children liked fall than liked spring?

Vocabulary

Which picture goes with each word?

1. hurricane
2. lightning
3. hibernate
4. migrate
5. tornado

A

B

C

D

E

What did you learn?

6. Tell what happens in each step of the water cycle.

7. Which season has the most daylight hours?

8. Collect Data Observe the weather for 10 days. Record the number of days that are sunny, cloudy, and rainy.

Draw Conclusions

9. Look at the picture. Which season do you think it is?

I know

My conclusion

Test Prep

Fill in the circle next to the correct answer.

10. When water vapor changes to liquid it _____.

  Ⓐ evaporates
  Ⓑ hibernates
  Ⓒ condenses
  Ⓓ migrates

11. **Writing** in Science

Write four sentences. Describe what the weather is like where you live in each of the four seasons.

Robbie Hood works as an Atmospheric Scientist at NASA.

Atmospheric Scientist

Read Together

Atmospheric scientists study the weather. Some atmospheric scientists who work at NASA study hurricanes. They want to learn more about how hurricanes work and what is the best way to use satellites to observe them.

Studying hurricanes has helped NASA scientists learn how to predict when and where a hurricane is likely to occur. This way, warnings can be given sooner and more people can move to places where they can stay safe.

Lab zone Take-Home Activity

Talk with your family about hurricanes. Make a list of reasons why atmospheric scientists are important people.

Chapter 7
Fossils and Dinosaurs

online
Student Edition
pearsonsuccessnet.com

You Will Discover

- what people can learn when they study fossils.
- what dinosaurs were like.

How can people learn about the Earth long ago?

dinosaur

fossil

202

Chapter 7 Vocabulary

fossil page 207

paleontologist page 207

extinct page 210

dinosaur page 212

extinct

paleontologist

203

Explore Which fossils match the plants and animals?

A fossil is a print or remains of a plant or animal that lived long ago.

Materials

puzzle cards

crayons or markers

scissors and glue

paper

What to Do

1 Cut out the cards.

Be careful!

Be careful with scissors.

Color the pictures.

2 Put the cards together. Match each fossil to an animal or a plant.

3 Glue the puzzles on paper.

Process Skills

You **communicate** when you answer questions.

Explain Your Results

Communicate How did you match fossils to plants and animals?

TARGET SKILL

Retell

Retell means to tell what you learned in your own words.

Science Story

Fossil Shell

Long ago, an animal lived in this huge fossil shell. The animal had long arms. Scientists think the arms had rows of suction cups just like an octopus.

Apply It!
Communicate
Tell what you learned about the animal in the fossil shell.

Retell

♪ Go Find a Fossil

Sung to the tune of "Take Me Out to the Ballgame"
Lyrics by Gerri Brioso & Richard Freitas/The Dovetail Group, Inc.

Take a shovel, go digging.
In the dirt you may find,
Rocks that have shapes printed right in them.
Shapes of a leaf or an animal!

If you find one, you have a fossil.
A special clue to the past.
See what plants and animals looked like
A long time ago!

How can we learn about the past?

A **fossil** is a print or remains of a plant or animal that lived long ago. Some fossils are very old bones. Other fossils are shapes left in rocks.

Scientists who study fossils are called **paleontologists.** Paleontologists use fossils to learn what plants and animals looked like long ago.

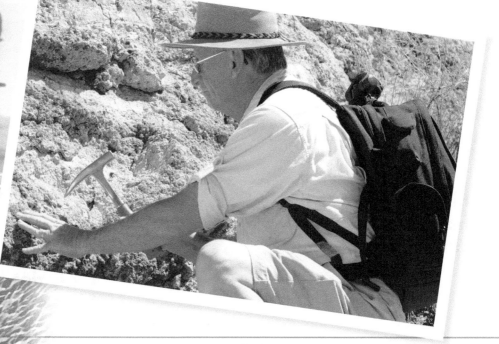

How Fossils Form

A fossil of a lizard has been left in a rock. The pictures on the next page show how one kind of fossil formed. Look at the other kinds of fossils on these pages.

This fossil shows the shape of another lizard that lived long ago.

Long ago, an animal made this footprint in the mud. The mud turned to rock. The footprint is another kind of fossil.

This shell is a fossil.

This fossil is of a plant that lived long ago.

✔ **Lesson Checkpoint**

1. What are fossils?

2. ↻ **Retell** how fossils are formed.

A Fossil Is Formed

A lizard dies.

The lizard is covered by sand and mud.

The sand and mud become rock. The print of the lizard is a fossil.

What can we learn from fossils?

Fossils show the size and shape of plants and animals that lived long ago. Some fossils are of plants and animals that are extinct. An **extinct** plant or animal no longer lives on Earth.

Todites denticulatus is an extinct plant. This fossil shows the shape of its leaves.

Sometimes plants and animals no longer get what they need from their habitat. The plants and animals cannot live. They may disappear from Earth forever.

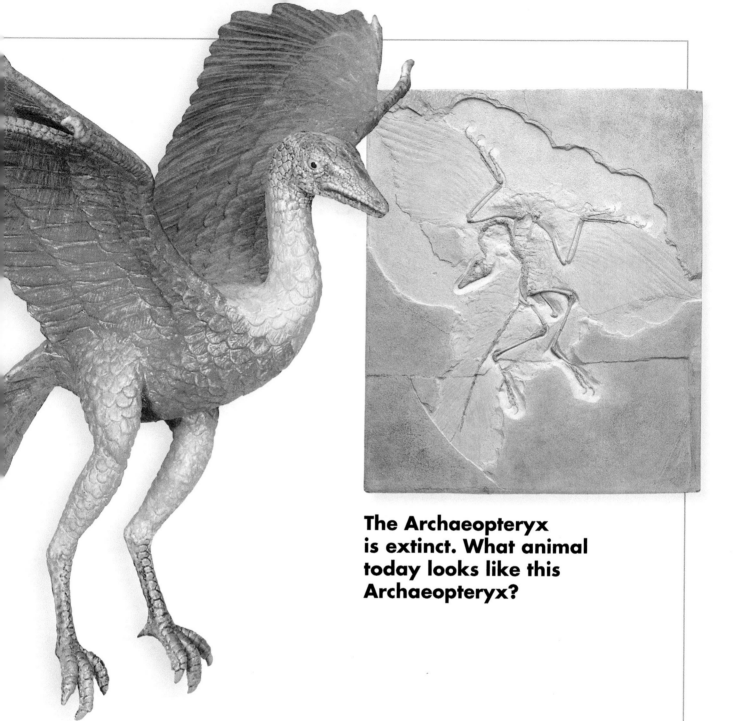

The Archaeopteryx is extinct. What animal today looks like this Archaeopteryx?

✓Lesson Checkpoint

1. What do paleontologists learn from fossils?

2. 🔄 **Retell** What can happen to plants and animals when they no longer get what they need from their habitat?

What were dinosaurs like?

Dinosaurs were animals that lived long ago. Some dinosaurs were very big. Other dinosaurs were small. Some dinosaurs ate plants. Some dinosaurs ate other animals. All dinosaurs are extinct.

A Compsognathus was about the same size as a chicken.

The Barosaurus was very tall.

Crunch!
The Iguanodon's big, flat teeth helped it chew plants.

Gulp!
A Dilophosaurus caught and ate other dinosaurs.

1. ✓ Checkpoint) What did an Iguanodon eat?

2. Writing in Science) Write about some ways dinosaurs were different. Tell how they are the same.

Learning About Dinosaurs

Paleontologists study fossils of dinosaur bones. They want to know what dinosaurs looked like. The Stegosaurus had a large body. Its head and mouth were small. Paleontologists think this dinosaur ate plants. A Stegosaurus needed an environment with lots of plants.

A Triceratops had three horns on its head! The horns may have helped stop other animals from attacking.

What big teeth! A Tyrannosaurus rex probably used its sharp teeth to eat meat.

Look at the skeleton of a Stegosaurus. Scientists used the skeleton to make a model of how the Stegosaurus may have looked.

✓ **Lesson Checkpoint**

1. What did paleontologists learn about a Stegosaurus by looking at its bones?

2. **Writing** in Science Write one sentence. Tell which dinosaur is your favorite and why.

What are some new discoveries?

An Oviraptor was a small dinosaur. Paleontologists found fossils of an Oviraptor near some eggs. They thought the Oviraptor was stealing the eggs to eat them.

Oviraptor eggs were twice as long as chicken eggs.

Later, another Oviraptor fossil was found. It was sitting on the same kind of eggs. Now paleontologists think that the Oviraptor was not stealing the eggs. They think the Oviraptor was keeping its own eggs safe.

1. What did paleontologists learn about the Oviraptor?

2. **Math** in Science Oviraptor eggs were about 20 centimeters long. Find something in your classroom that you think is about 20 centimeters long. Measure it.

Paleontologists now think that Oviraptors kept their eggs safe from other animals.

Guided Inquiry

Investigate How can you make a model of a fossil?

Materials

shell

clay

2 classroom objects

What to Do

1 **Make a model** of a fossil. Press a shell into clay.

2 Tell about your fossil model and the shell.

How the Fossil Model and the Shell Are Alike and Different	
How are they alike?	**How are they different?**

③ Now pick an object in your classroom. Make a fossil model of the object.

④ **Observe** your partner's fossil model. Guess what it is.

Explain Your Results

1. How did you **infer** what your partner's fossil model was?
2. How do fossils give clues about living things?

Go Further

What else could you do to make models of fossils? Make a plan and try it.

Math in Science

Measuring Fossil Leaves

Look at the fossils of 3 leaves. Estimate how long each leaf is in centimeters. Measure the leaves.

1

2

3

eTools Take It to the Net
pearsonsuccessnet.com

Make a bar graph like this one. Fill in the graph to show how long each leaf is. Use your bar graph to answer the questions.

1. Which leaf is the longest?

2. Which leaf is the shortest?

3. How much longer is the longest leaf than the shortest leaf?

Fossil Leaves

Length in Centimeters

15
14
13
12
11
10
9
8
7
6
5
4
3
2
1
0

① ② ③

Leaves

Vocabulary

Which picture goes with each word?

1. paleontologist
2. fossil
3. dinosaur

What did you learn?

4. Why do some plants and animals become extinct?

5. How does a leaf fossil form?

6. How can people use fossils to learn about the past?

7. Communicate Tell how fossils help us learn what some dinosaurs were like.

⊙ Retell

8.

A Triceratops' head could grow up to 7 feet long. It had a bird-like beak to help it eat plants.

Retell what you learned about the Triceratops.

Retell

Test Prep

Fill in the circle next to the correct answer.

9. Which dinosaur was as tall as a chicken?

Ⓐ Tyrannosaurus
Ⓑ Barosaurus
Ⓒ Compsognathus
Ⓓ Archaeopteryx

10. Writing in Science Write two sentences. Tell what you learned about paleontologists.

A Tyrannosaurus rex skeleton

Susan Hendrickson

Read Together

How would you like to have a dinosaur named after you? This Tyrannosaurus rex is named Sue. It is named after Susan Hendrickson. Susan Hendrickson is a paleontologist. She looks for extinct animals to show in museums.

Susan Hendrickson found the fossil bones of this Tyrannosaurus rex. You can see Sue the Tyrannosaurus rex if you visit the Field Museum in Chicago.

Lab zone Take-Home Activity

Use pipe cleaners to make a model of a Tyrannosaurus rex skeleton. Share your model with your family.

Unit B Test Talk

Use Information from Text and Graphics

You can use information from text and charts to help you answer science questions.

Month	Rainfall
March	1 inch
April	4 inches
May	3 inches

March had the least rain. The months of April and May had more rain than March.

Use the information from the text and the chart to answer the question.

Which month had the most rain?

Ⓐ March

Ⓑ April

Ⓒ May

Ⓓ June

The text tells that April and May had more rain than March. Look at the chart. Which month had the most rain?

225

Unit B Wrap-Up

Chapter 5

What are Earth's natural resources?
- Sunlight, air, and water are some of Earth's natural resources.

Chapter 6

How does weather change?
- Weather can change from day to day.
- Different seasons have different kinds of weather.

Chapter 7

How can people learn about Earth long ago?
- People study fossils to learn about plants and animals that lived on Earth long ago.

Performance Assessment

Make a model of water erosion.

- Put some sandbox sand on a cookie pan.
- Tilt the pan slightly.
- Slowly pour water from a cup at the top of the pan.
- Watch the water erode the sand.
- Tell how you could keep the sand from eroding.

Read More about Earth Science!

Experiment Does gravel, sand, or soil make the best imprint?

Sometimes sand can slowly change to rock. An imprint made by a plant or animal can become a fossil in the rock.

Materials

safety goggles

3 paper plates

3 index cards

cup with gravel,
cup with sand,
cup with soil

shell

Process Skills

A **hypothesis** answers a question that you can test.

Ask a question.
Which will make the best imprint?

Make your hypothesis.
Is the best imprint made in gravel, sand, or soil? Tell what you think.

Plan a fair test.
Use the same amount on each plate.

Do your test.

1 Put gravel, sand or soil on each plate.

Label each plate.

sand

soil

gravel

2 Press the shell into the gravel, sand, or soil.

Wash your hands when you are finished.

3 **Observe** the imprint in each pile.

Collect and record data.
Fill in the chart. Use an **X.**

Which is the best imprint?			
	Best Imprint	**Some Imprint**	**No Imprint**
Gravel			
Sand			
Soil			

Tell your conclusion.
Does gravel, sand, or soil make the best imprint? Which would make the best imprint fossil?

Go Further
What might happen if you use wet sand, soil, and gravel? Try it and find out.

A Wildflower Meadow

See the carpet of colorful flowers
and green-gold feathery grasses,
all gently waving
as the spring wind passes.

A home to bumblebees and birds,
frogs and moths and butterflies,
the springtime wildflower meadow
is quite a special prize.

While it's true that many plants
have a special duty,
the gift of a wildflower meadow
is its amazing beauty.

Science Fair Projects

Full Inquiry

Using Scientific Methods

1. Ask a question.
2. Make a hypothesis.
3. Plan a fair test.
4. Do your test.
5. Collect and record data.
6. Tell your conclusions.
7. Go further.

Idea 1
How Fast Water Evaporates

Plan a project. Find out if water evaporates faster in a cold place or a warm place.

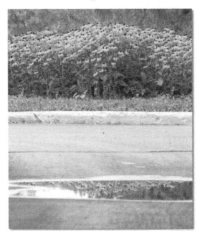

Idea 2
Measuring Temperature

Plan a project. Find out how the temperature outside changes during the day.

Unit C

Physical Science

Chapter 8 Properties of Matter

Directed Inquiry   What happens when oil is mixed with water?

Guided Inquiry   How can water change?

Activity Flip Chart   How are solids different from liquids?
How can you make an ice cube melt faster?

Quick Activity
Transparencies   What is matter?
What is solid water like?
How can you change matter?
How does temperature change matter?

Chapter 9 Energy

Directed Inquiry   Which color heats faster?

Guided Inquiry   How can you change light?

Activity Flip Chart   How does electricity make a light bulb light up?
What gives off heat?

Quick Activity
Transparencies   What is energy?
What gives you energy?
What causes heat?
How does light move?
What is energy of motion?

Chapter 10 Forces and Motion

Directed Inquiry   How can you measure force?

Guided Inquiry   What can magnets do?

Activity Flip Chart   Do heavy objects fall faster than light objects?
How do objects move on different surfaces?

Quick Activity
Transparencies   How do objects move?
When does work happen?
How can you change the way things move?
How can tools help you do work?
What are magnets?

Chapter 11 Sound

Directed Inquiry   How can you make sound?

Guided Inquiry   How can you change sound?

Activity Flip Chart   How can you describe sound?
How does sound travel?

Quick Activity
Transparencies   What is sound?
What is pitch?
How does sound travel?
How do some animals make sounds?
What are some sounds around you?

Unit C

Full Inquiry   What kinds of objects reflect light clearly?

STEM Project   The Inclined Plane

Chapter 8
Properties of Matter

You Will Discover

- the three states of matter.
- ways that matter can be changed.

Web Games
Take It to the Net
pearsonsuccessnet.com

online
Student Edition

pearsonsuccessnet.com

What are some properties of matter?

property

liquid

mass

gas

234

states of matter

solid

mixture

Chapter 8 Vocabulary

mass page 239

property page 240

states of matter page 242

solid page 242

liquid page 244

gas page 246

mixture page 250

235

Lab zone — Directed Inquiry

Explore What happens when oil is mixed with water?

Materials

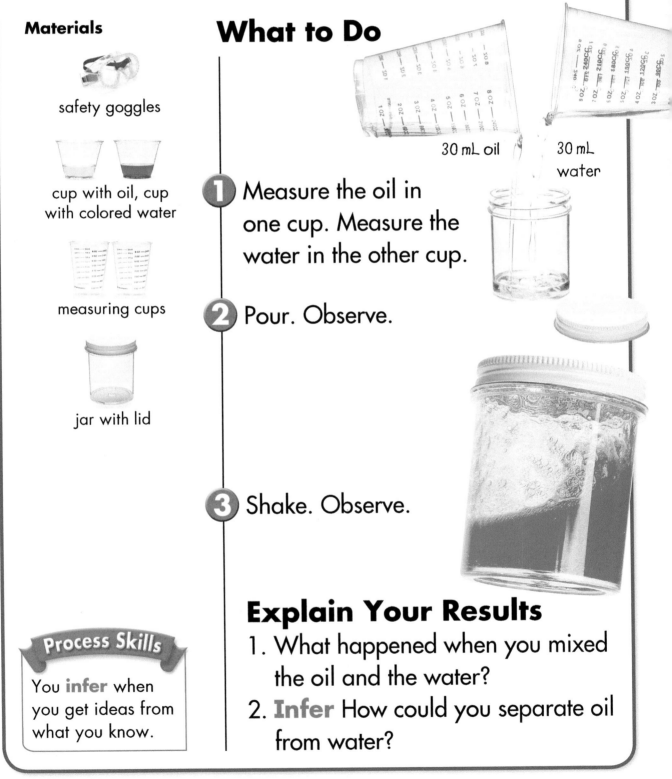

safety goggles

cup with oil, cup with colored water

measuring cups

jar with lid

What to Do

30 mL oil

30 mL water

1. Measure the oil in one cup. Measure the water in the other cup.

2. Pour. Observe.

3. Shake. Observe.

Explain Your Results

1. What happened when you mixed the oil and the water?
2. **Infer** How could you separate oil from water?

Process Skills

You **infer** when you get ideas from what you know.

How to Read Science

Reading Skills

TARGET SKILL Draw Conclusions

You draw conclusions when you decide about something you see or read.

Science Activity

Work with a partner. You will need one cup with water and one cup with sand. Mix the sand into the water. Record the results in your science journal.

Apply It!

Infer What do you think will happen when you mix the sand and the water?

I know.

My conclusion.

 →

♪ They're All Matter!

Sung to the tune of "Old MacDonald"
Lyrics by Gerri Brioso & Richard Freitas/The Dovetail Group, Inc.

Anything that takes up space
Is made up of matter.
Anything that has some mass
Is made up of matter.
Teddy bears, a crayon box,
Watermelon, rocking chairs,
  every wall around you
All have mass and take up space.
That's why they're all matter.

Lesson 1

What is matter?

Matter is anything that takes up space and has mass. **Mass** is the amount of matter in an object.

Look around your classroom. Everything you see is made of matter.

Some things you cannot see are made of matter. The air around you has matter.

Matter is made of very small parts. You can use a hand lens to take a closer look at things.

Properties of Matter

All matter has properties. A **property** is something that you can observe with your senses. Some properties of matter are color, shape, and size. Mass is a property of matter. How something feels is a property of matter.

Is the brush hard or soft? Is the cup smooth or rough?

What colors are the pipe cleaners?

This clip is blue and silver. This clip feels smooth.

Do you think the sponge is heavy or light? Does it float or sink? Whether an object sinks or floats is a property.

✓ Lesson Checkpoint

1. What are some properties of matter?

2. **Math** in Science Tell four ways you can sort objects using properties.

Lesson 2

What are the states of matter?

You know that everything around you is made of matter. The three **states of matter** are solids, liquids, and gases.

A **solid** is matter that has its own size and shape. Solids take up space and have mass.

Paintbrushes are solids. What are some properties of this paintbrush?

You can use a balance to measure the mass of a solid.

The box and the things in it are solids. Each thing has its own size, shape, and mass.

Crayons are solids. What are some properties of the crayons?

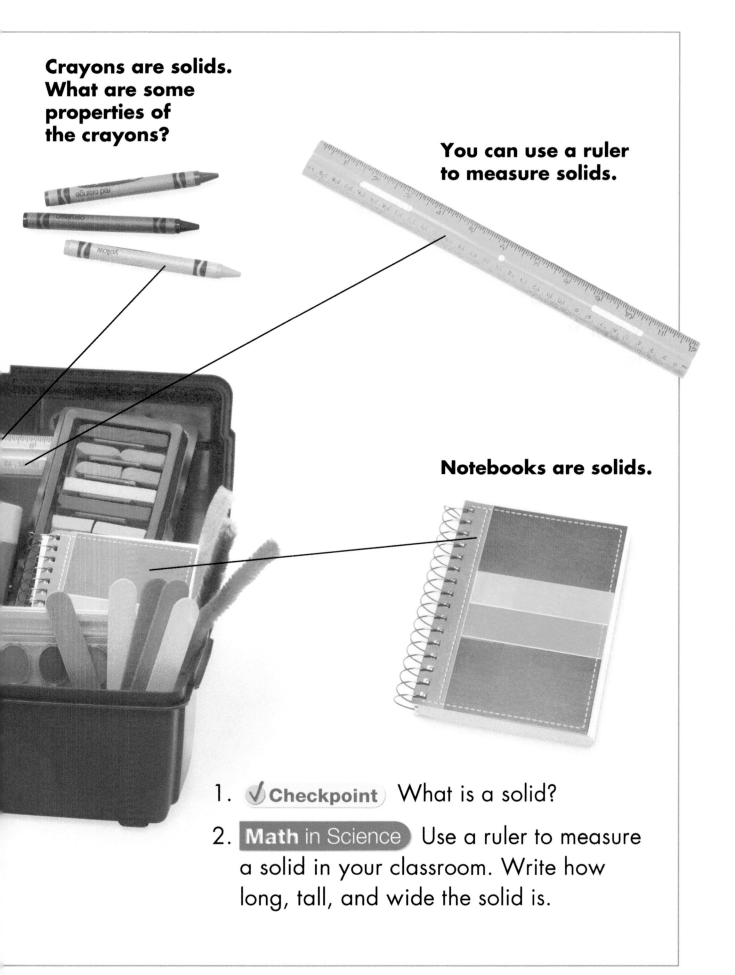

You can use a ruler to measure solids.

Notebooks are solids.

1. ✓ **Checkpoint** What is a solid?

2. **Math** in Science Use a ruler to measure a solid in your classroom. Write how long, tall, and wide the solid is.

Liquids

A **liquid** is matter that does not have its own shape. Liquids take the shape of their containers.

Liquids take up space and have mass. Water is a liquid. Pour water into a jar. The water takes the same shape as the jar.

One way to measure liquids is to use a measuring cup. The amount of space a liquid takes up is called *volume*.

1. ✓Checkpoint What is a liquid?

2. **Writing** in Science Write 2 sentences about solids and liquids in your **science journal.** Tell how solids and liquids are alike and different.

Gases

A **gas** is matter that does not have its own shape or size. Gas takes the size and shape of its container. Gas always takes up all the space inside its container. Gas can change size and shape. Gas has mass.

The bubble is filled with gas. Gas takes the size and shape of the bubble.

These balloons are filled with gas. Gas takes the size and shape of the balloons.

Breathe in. Breathe out. The air
you breathe is made of gases.

✓ **Lesson Checkpoint**

1. What are some properties of gases?

2. 🎯 **Draw Conclusions** Is there
   more gas in a full balloon or an empty
   balloon? Write a sentence to explain
   your answer.

How can matter be changed?

Matter can be changed. Different matter changes in different ways. You can change the size of matter. You can change the shape of matter.

You can fold paper to give it a new shape.

You can mold clay to give it a new shape.

1. ✓**Checkpoint** Name 3 ways that you can change the size or shape of matter.

2. 🎯 **Draw Conclusions** What might happen to wood if you cut it? How might it change?

You can tear paper to change its size.

You can bend a pipe cleaner to change its shape.

Mixing and Separating Matter

A **mixture** is something made up of two or more kinds of matter. Matter in a mixture does not change. This fruit salad is a mixture.

You can separate a mixture to see its parts. Suppose you separate the fruits in the salad. Each piece of fruit will stay the same.

Look at the pictures. One mixture is made with sand and water. One mixture is made with salt and water. There are different ways to separate these mixtures. You can let the matter sink. You can let the water evaporate.

Mixing with Water

Look at this mixture. It is easy to see the sand and the water.

Look at the cup on the left. It has a mixture of salt and water. Look at the cup on the right. What happened after the water evaporated?

✓ Lesson Checkpoint

1. What are 2 ways to separate a mixture?

2. **Art** in Science Draw 2 things being mixed. How could you separate the mixture? Draw it.

Liquid water is poured into a plastic tray. The tray is put in a freezer. The water will change to ice.

Lesson 4

How can cooling and heating change matter?

Water is matter. Water can change. Suppose the temperature of water is below 0° Celsius. The water will freeze. The water will change to ice. Ice is solid water.

Water can change from a gas to a liquid.
Water as a gas is called water vapor.

Water vapor in the air touches the cold glass. The water vapor changes from a gas to liquid. Tiny drops of water form on the glass.

Rain will freeze if the air temperature is very cold. Water on these leaves changed from a liquid to a solid.

1. ✓ **Checkpoint** How can you change water from a liquid to a solid?

2. **Math** in Science At what temperature does water become a solid?

Heating Matter

Heating can change the state of matter. Heat can change solids to liquids. Heat can change liquids to gases.

Ice and snow melt when the air warms. Solid water becomes liquid.

Heat from sunlight evaporates water. The liquid water changes to a gas.

When you boil water, the liquid water becomes a gas. This gas is called water vapor.

Heat changes other matter from solids to liquids. Butter melts when you heat it. What are some ways that you can use melted butter?

✓ **Lesson Checkpoint**

1. How can heat change water?

2. **Writing** in Science Write 3 sentences in your **science journal.** Describe water as a solid, a liquid, and a gas.

Investigate How can water change?

You can see water in many forms. Rain is liquid water. Ice is solid water.

Materials

cup with water

thermometer

What to Do

1 **Observe** Describe the liquid water. **Measure** the temperature.

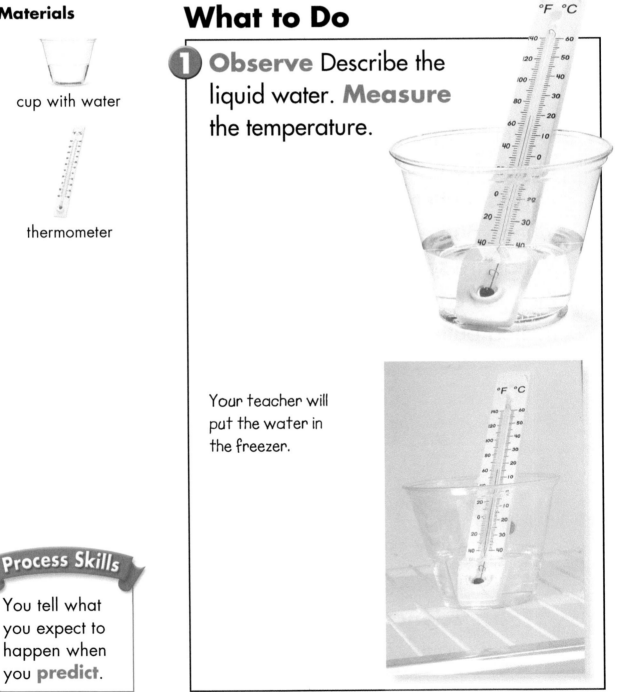

Your teacher will put the water in the freezer.

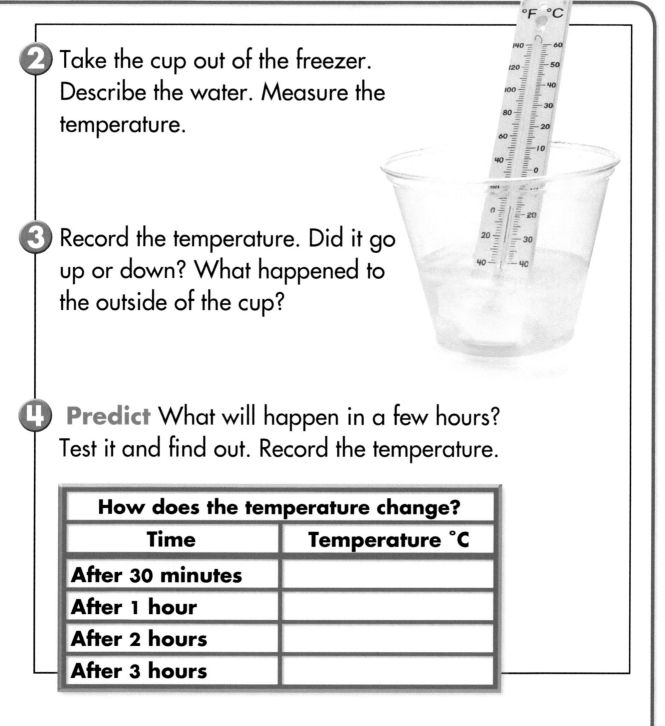

2 Take the cup out of the freezer. Describe the water. Measure the temperature.

3 Record the temperature. Did it go up or down? What happened to the outside of the cup?

4 **Predict** What will happen in a few hours? Test it and find out. Record the temperature.

| How does the temperature change? ||
Time	Temperature °C
After 30 minutes	
After 1 hour	
After 2 hours	
After 3 hours	

Explain Your Results

1. Compare solid water to liquid water.
2. **Predict** How long would it take for the liquid water to evaporate? Try it and find out.

Go Further

What other kinds of matter change when they are frozen? Investigate to find out.

Math in Science

How Can You Measure Matter?

Collect these tools for measuring.

Collect each pair of objects.

Estimate the length of each book. Use a ruler to measure the length of each book in centimeters.

Estimate the volume of each cup. Use a measuring cup to measure the water in each glass. Use milliliters.

Estimate the mass of each balloon. Use a balance to measure the mass of each balloon in grams.

Measure each pair of objects.
Record your data in a chart.

My Measurements

Length	Volume	Mass
1. ___ cm	1. ___ ml	1. ___ g
2. ___ cm	2. ___ ml	2. ___ g

Lab zone Take-Home Activity

Measure things at home. Use paper clips to measure length. Use a drinking glass to measure volume. Use your hands like a balance to estimate mass.

Vocabulary

Which picture goes with each word?

1. solid

2. gas

3. mixture

4. liquid

What did you learn?

5. What are three states of matter?

6. Name two ways to change properties of paper.

7. Observe Look around your classroom. Tell one way that matter in your classroom can be changed.

☉ Draw Conclusions

8. Draw Conclusions What made the candle change? Fill in the graphic organizer.

I Know.   Conclusion.

Test Prep

Fill in the circle next to the correct answer.

9. Which state of matter has its own shape and size?
  Ⓐ solid
  Ⓑ liquid
  Ⓒ gas
  Ⓓ property

10. Writing in Science Choose a solid in your classroom. Describe its properties.

Space Food

Astronauts in space need to take their food with them. Scientists have found a way to make taking food in space easier. Many foods contain water. Taking the water out of foods helps in space travel. Foods with no water have less mass.

Taking the water out of foods means the food takes up less space. Some examples of food astronauts take into space are soup, macaroni and cheese, and scrambled eggs. Before astronauts eat this food, they have to put the water back in. When the water is mixed back in, the foods taste good.

Lab zone Take-Home Activity

What are some kinds of food or drink you make at home by adding water? How do you change the matter?

Material Scientist

Read Together

Material scientists study the properties of different kinds of matter. Some material scientists work at NASA.

Material scientists work to make things that can hold matter that is very hot. Material scientists at NASA also work to make things that will not break in space.

Narrottam Bansal is a material scientist. He works at NASA.

Lab zone Take-Home Activity

Which kind of matter can hold a spoon when it is wet? Try a tissue, a paper towel, and a piece of cloth. Tell your family what you learned.

You Will Discover
- what energy is.
- why energy is important.

Chapter 9

Energy

What are some kinds of energy?

energy

solar energy

266

source

fuel

Chapter 9 Vocabulary

energy page 271

solar energy page 272

source page 278

fuel page 279

conductor page 281

reflect page 282

shadow page 284

reflect

conductor

shadow

Explore Which color heats faster?

Materials

2 thermometers

black and white paper

tape

What to Do

1 Wrap thermometers.

Fold. Tape.

Put the wrapped thermometers in the sun.

2 Wait 1 hour. Read the temperatures.

Process Skills

When you **infer**, you use what you observe to answer a question.

Explain Your Results

Infer How did color make a difference in temperature?

How to Read Science

TARGET SKILL

Infer

Infer means to use what you know to answer a question.

Science Story

Tom and Ramon play after school every day. Today they are playing football. It is a hot and sunny day.

Apply It!

Infer Which child will feel warmer?

I know.   I can infer.

269

Where Do We Get Energy?

Sung to the tune of "Billy Boy"
Lyrics by Gerri Brioso & Richard Freitas/The Dovetail Group, Inc.

Oh, where do we get energy, energy?
Oh, where do we get energy?
We get most of it from the Sun.
So there's heat for everyone.
Yes we get lots of energy from the Sun.

Science Songs

Lesson 1
What is energy?

Anything that can do work and cause change has **energy.** You use energy when you do work or play. You use energy when you are awake. You use energy when you are asleep. You use energy when you walk, run, or breathe.

Energy from the Sun

Earth gets most of its energy from the Sun. Heat from the Sun warms the land, air, and water on Earth. **Solar energy** is heat and light from the Sun.

People and animals use sunlight to see in the daytime. Earth would stay dark without the Sun.

This black glass panel collects solar energy to heat this home.

✓ Lesson Checkpoint

1. Where does Earth get most of its energy?

2. **Writing** in Science Make a list. What things give us light? What things give us heat?

How do living things use energy?

Most living things need energy from the Sun. Green leaves on plants use sunlight, air, water, and nutrients to make food. Plants use the food to live and grow.

Animals use energy to live and grow. Animals get energy from the food they eat. The food comes from plants or from animals that eat plants. The plants get energy from the Sun. People need energy too.

1. ✓ Checkpoint How is energy from the Sun important to plants?

2. 🎯 Infer How do you think people get and use energy?

275

How People Get Energy

Food gives you energy to work and play. Food gives you energy to grow.

The pictures show five food groups. You should eat foods from each food group every day. Eating food from these food groups can help you grow and stay healthy. Be careful not to eat too many sweets or foods with a lot of fat.

✓ **Lesson Checkpoint**

1. Name the five important food groups.

2. **Health** in Science Plan a healthful lunch. Be sure to choose something from each food group.

Vegetables

Vegetables have many vitamins your body needs.

Bread, Rice, Cereal, and Pasta

The foods in this group help give you energy.

Meat, Fish, Eggs, Dry Beans

The foods in this group have nutrients that help your body grow and stay strong.

Fruit

Fruit has many vitamins and minerals that can help you stay healthy.

Milk, Yogurt, Cheese

The foods in this group are important for healthy bones and teeth.

277

Lesson 3

What are some sources of heat?

Sunlight is one source of heat. A **source** is a place from which something comes. Sunlight warms Earth.

Heat comes from other sources too. What other sources of heat do you see in the pictures?

Rubbing your hands together can make your hands feel warmer.

You can feel heat from a candle.

278

The picture of the campfire shows wood burning. Wood is a kind of fuel. **Fuel** is something that is burned to make heat. Coal, gas, and oil are other kinds of fuels.

✔ Checkpoint

1. What are some sources of heat?

2. Social Studies in Science Look at a map of the United States. In which parts of the country do people need to use the most fuel to heat their homes?

Fire is a source of heat.

How Heat Moves

Heat moves from warmer objects and places to cooler ones. People can use heat to cook. Look at the picture. Heat moves from the hot burner on the stove to the pan. Then heat moves from the hot pan to the cold food.

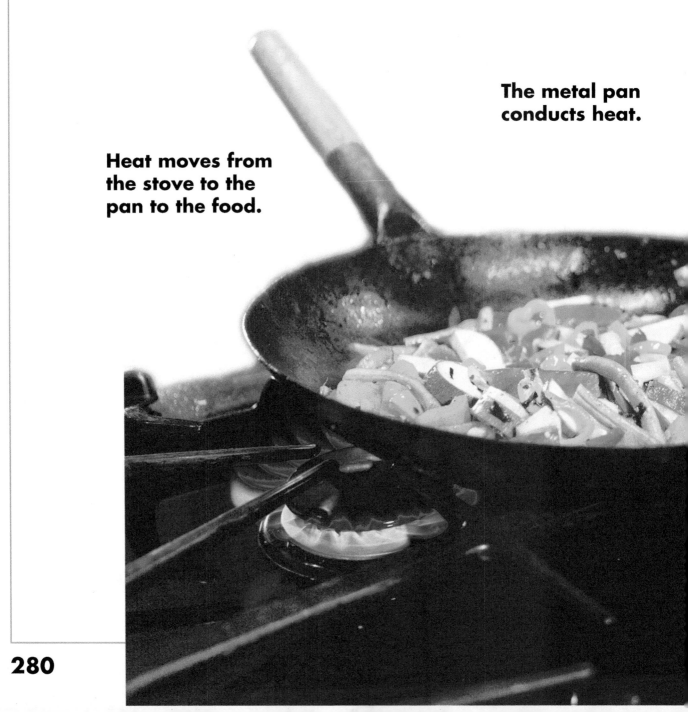

The metal pan conducts heat.

Heat moves from the stove to the pan to the food.

How do you boil water?

Fill a pot with water. The pot and the water are cool. Put the pot on the stove. Heat moves from the stove to the pot. Then the heat moves from the pot to the water. The heat makes the water hot enough to boil.

The pan in the picture is metal. Metal is a conductor. A **conductor** is something that lets heat easily move through it. Some materials are not good conductors. Wood and cloth are not good conductors. Heat does not move easily through wood and cloth.

✔ Lesson Checkpoint

1. Why are many pans made of metal?

2. Writing in Science Make a list. What things conduct heat well? What things do not conduct heat well?

Lesson 4
How does light move?

Light is a form of energy. The Sun, a lamp, a flashlight, and a fire are sources of light. Most light sources give off heat too. Light moves in straight lines. Light can move through some things such as clear glass.

Light **reflects** when it bounces off something. Light reflects well from smooth, shiny things such as a mirror. The picture shows how light reflects.

Most of the light you see is white light. The rainbow shows the colors that make up white light. Raindrops in the air can bend sunlight. Then the sunlight is separated into the colors in a rainbow.

Dark colors take in light. You might feel warm when you wear dark colors in the sunlight. Light colors reflect the sunlight. You can stay cooler when you wear light colors.

The colors in a rainbow are red, orange, yellow, green, blue, and violet.

Light colors help you stay cool in warm weather.

1. ✔ Checkpoint How is a rainbow made?
2. Art in Science Use crayons to show the six colors in a rainbow.

Shadows

A **shadow** is made when something blocks the light. You can see your shadow when your body blocks the sunlight.

Shadows change during the day. The Sun looks low in the sky in early morning. Shadows look long. The Sun looks high in the sky in the middle of the day. Shadows look short.

Shadows are long in the morning when the Sun rises. They get shorter until noon.

Shadows are shortest at noon. Then they grow longer until sunset.

You can use a flashlight to make shadows. Block the light with a shape cut from paper. Move the shape away from or toward the light. You can make the size of the shadow change.

✓ Lesson Checkpoint

1. Suppose you are standing outside on a sunny day. When would your shadow be the shortest?

2. **Math** in Science A shadow is 200 cm at breakfast, 100 cm at morning recess, and 50 cm at lunch. What pattern do you see?

Lesson 5

What are other kinds of energy?

You use different kinds of energy every day. Look at the picture of the grocery cart. You could push the cart to make it move. The moving cart would have energy of motion.

Wind is another kind of energy. Look at the picture of the boat. Wind energy can make the boat move.

Look at the musical instruments in the picture. What sounds do the instruments make? Sound is a kind of energy.

√ Checkpoint

1. What are some other kinds of energy?

2. **Social Studies** in Science   Look at a map of the United States. Where might you be able to sail a boat?

Using Electricity Safely

What happens when you turn on a light? Electricity makes the light work. What other things in your home use electricity? What kinds of things at school use electricity?

Batteries can help provide electricity.

A lamp and a clock use electricity.

Electricity Safety Tips

- **Keep things that use electricity away from water.**

- **Do not put too many plugs into outlets.**

- **Do not pull on cords to unplug things. Hold onto the plug.**

- **Do not touch cords that have wire showing.**

- **Do not play near power lines.**

It is important to use electricity safely. The chart tells you how to stay safe when using electricity.

✓ **Lesson Checkpoint**

1. What is one way you can stay safe around electricity?

2. **Infer** Why shouldn't you use a hair dryer in the bathroom?

Lab zone Guided Inquiry

Investigate How can you change light?

Materials

mirror

tub with water

flashlight

posterboard

crayons or markers

What to Do

1 Hold a mirror on one side of the tub. Ask a partner to shine light on the mirror. Your partner should hold the posterboard behind the flashlight.

2 Tilt the mirror to shine the light on the posterboard.

3 **Observe.** Draw what you see.

Changing Light

Process Skills

You **observe** the colors that the light and water make.

What colors do you see?

Explain Your Results

1. What are some of the colors you saw?

2. **Infer** How does the light change when it passes through water?

Go Further

How would using colored paper change the colors you see? Try it and find out.

291

Measuring Shadows

How does sunlight change a shadow during the day?

1. Put a pencil in clay outside on a sunny day.
2. Measure the shadow in the morning. Record.
3. Measure the shadow at lunch. Record.
4. Measure the shadow at the end of the school day. Record.
5. Tell how the length of the shadow changes during the day.

Changing Shadows

Time of day	morning	lunch	end of day
Shadow length			

Lab zone **Take-Home Activity**

Have someone measure your shadow at different times during the day. Write down what you find. Tell how your shadow changes as the Sun moves.

Vocabulary

Which picture goes with each word?

1. solar energy
2. fuel
3. reflect

What did you learn?

4. How do people get energy?

5. Name four kinds of energy.

6. What conducts energy better, a metal pan or a wooden spoon?

7. Observe a shadow outside your classroom window. How does the shadow change during the day?

◎ Infer

8. Infer Look at the shadow of the tree. What time of day do you think it is?

I know.   I can infer.

Test Prep

Fill in the circle that correctly answers the question.

9. Where does Earth get most of its energy?

Ⓐ from food
Ⓑ from the Moon
Ⓒ from the Sun
Ⓓ from wind

10. Writing in Science Describe two kinds of energy. Tell how they are important to you.

Lights, Camera, Action!
Lighting Operator

Read Together

Do you know what a gaffer is? Have you heard of a best boy? They are people who work with the lights on a movie set. A gaffer is a lighting operator. A best boy helps the lighting operator.

Lighting operators use lights to make it look cloudy when it is sunny. They can also make it look bright when the sky is dark.

Lighting operators use lights to make it look very bright on the movie set.

Lab zone Take-Home Activity

You can use a lamp to help you see in the dark. Draw a picture of one more thing that you could use for light when it is dark.

296

You Will Discover

- that objects can move in different ways.
- that force causes objects to move.

Chapter 10

Forces and Motion

online
Student Edition
pearsonsuccessnet.com

How do forces cause objects to move?

motion

gravity

force

work

friction

simple machine

298

Chapter 10 Vocabulary

motion page 303

force page 304

gravity page 306

work page 308

friction page 312

simple machine page 314

attract page 318

repel page 318

attract

S N

repel

N N

Explore How can you measure force?

You use force when you pull and push things.
Force can be measured.

Materials

safety goggles

rubber band and string

2 books

ruler

What to Do

1 Pull the rubber band to move the book. **Measure** how long the rubber band is when you pull it.

When the rubber band gets longer, more force is being used.

Be careful! Wear your safety goggles!

2 Add 1 more book. Pull and measure.

Process Skills

You share information with your classmates when you **communicate**.

Explain Your Results

Communicate How are the measurements different?

How to Read Science

TARGET SKILL

Put Things in Order

When you put things in order, you tell what happens first, next, and last.

Science Story

Books!

Tony went to a used book sale in his neighborhood.
He saw so many books he wanted to buy!
Tony used his wagon to take all of his books home.

Apply It!

Communicate Look at the pictures. Tell how to put the pictures in order to tell what happened first, next, and last. Use the story to help you.

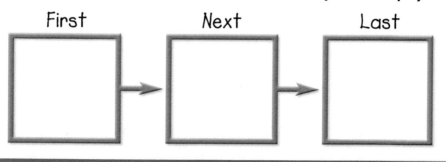

First   Next   Last

301

Use Some Force!

Sung to the tune of "If You're Happy"
Lyrics by Gerri Brioso & Richard Freitas/The Dovetail Group, Inc.

If you want to move the ball,
Use some force.
If you want to move the ball,
Use some force.
If you want it to go far,
Kick it hard and there you are.
You just moved the ball by using lots of force.

Science Songs

How do objects move?

Motion is the act of moving. Objects can move in different ways. Push a toy truck across the floor. The truck can move in a straight line. Move the truck in a zigzag motion. This means you push the truck in one direction and then another direction.

A swing moves back and forth. The merry-go-round in the picture moves around and around.

Force

You can move things in different ways. A push or a pull that makes something move is called a **force.** A force can change the way an object moves.

You use force to move a wagon.

An object will move in the direction it is pushed or pulled. Pull on the wagon. The wagon will move forward.

SciLinks   Take It to the Net
pearsonsuccessnet.com   keyword: force
code: g2p301

An object moves faster when you apply more force. The swing will move faster if you push it with more force.

You need to apply more force to move heavier objects than lighter ones. Would you need more force to move a book or a pencil?

The boy gives the swing a push.

1. ✔ Checkpoint What is force?

2. Writing in Science Write a sentence in your **science journal.** Tell about something you need force to do.

Gravity

The children in the picture are throwing leaves into the air. What will happen to the leaves? Gravity will pull the leaves down. **Gravity** is a force. Gravity pulls things toward the center of Earth.

Suppose you jump up in the air. What will happen? Gravity will pull you down to Earth. If you let go of an object, gravity will pull it down to Earth too.

Throw a basketball up to the hoop. Gravity pulls it down. Swoosh!

✓ Lesson Checkpoint

1. Why do you come down after you jump up?

2. 🎯 **Put Things in Order** Suppose you wanted to throw a basketball through a hoop. Put the steps you should follow in order.

307

What is work?

Suppose you push a crayon across the desk. You use force to move the crayon. **Work** happens whenever a force makes an object move. You do work when you push the crayon across the desk.

The amount of work you do depends on how much force you use and how far the object moves. It does not take much work to move the crayon across the desk. It takes a lot of work to push this bobsled up the hill.

If an object does not move, no work is done. Push hard against a wall. You are not doing work because the wall does not move.

This boy cannot move the haybale. He is not doing work.

✔ **Lesson Checkpoint**

1. How can you tell if you are doing work?

2. **Writing** in Science Make a list in your **science journal.** Write down five kinds of work you do each day.

Tap!

Lesson 3

How can you change the way things move?

You know that a force can change the way an object moves. A moving object that is pushed or pulled will speed up, slow down, or change direction.

How can you make a soccer ball roll just a little bit? How can you make it roll farther? It depends on how much force you use. Tap a soccer ball gently. It will not go far.

Kick a soccer ball harder. It will move farther. It takes more force to move objects farther.

Suppose you change the direction of the force. The soccer ball will move in a different direction. Someone kicks the soccer ball to you. The ball changes direction when you kick it back.

Bam!

1. ✓**Checkpoint** How can the amount of force used change the way an object moves?

2. **Math** in Science Push a book across the floor. Measure how far it goes. Push it harder. Measure how far it goes. Compare the results.

Friction

Think about rolling a ball across a field. Why does the ball stop moving? **Friction** is a force that makes moving objects slow down or stop moving.

Look at the bicycles in these pictures. A bicycle will move faster on a smooth road than it will on grass. The friction between the bicycle tires and the grass will make the bicycle slow down.

Rub your hands together. Your hands feel warm. Objects become warm when they rub together. Friction causes heat.

✓ **Lesson Checkpoint**

1. How does friction change the motion of an object?

2. 🔄 **Put Things in Order** You want to ride your bike. Put the steps you should follow in order.

312

How can simple machines help you do work?

Suppose you want to move an object. You might use a tool to help you. A machine is a tool that can make work easier. A **simple machine** is a tool with few or no moving parts.

A wheel and axle is a simple machine. A wheel and axle can help you move things.

A wedge is a simple machine that is used to push things apart.

A screw is a simple machine. A screw is used to hold things together.

A lever is a simple machine. It is used to move things. This screwdriver is used as a lever.

An inclined plane is a simple machine. An inclined plane makes it easier to move things.

A pulley is a simple machine. Pulleys move an object up, down, or sideways.

1. ✔Checkpoint You have to move some heavy boxes. Which simple machines could you use?

2. **Social Studies** in Science
What kinds of transportation use a wheel and axle?

Animal Body Parts

Think about different kinds of animals. Some kinds of animals dig into the ground. Birds use their beaks to get food. Some body parts of animals are like simple machines. Animals use these body parts to do work.

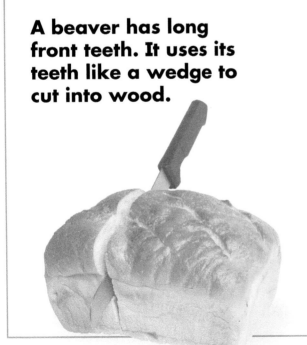

A beaver has long front teeth. It uses its teeth like a wedge to cut into wood.

This bird's beak is like a lever. This bird uses its beak to scoop fish from the water.

1. How are a beaver's teeth like a simple machine?

2. **Technology** in Science Name some tools you use that are simple machines.

Badger claws are like wedges. The claws help the badger dig into the ground.

A rabbit can use its claws as wedges to dig into the ground. It can then use its claws and hind feet like shovels, or levers, to lift the dirt out.

Lesson 5

What are magnets?

Magnets can push or pull certain metal objects. Magnets attract some metal objects. **Attract** means to pull toward. Magnets can repel other magnets. **Repel** means to push away.

Where have you seen magnets?

These magnets are attached to colorful letters and shapes.

Magnets have poles. The N stands for north pole. The S stands for south pole. A pole is the place on a magnet that has the strongest push or pull.

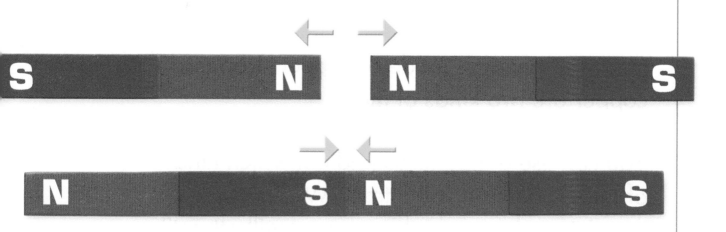

Like poles will repel when you put them together. The magnets will push away from each other. Opposite poles will attract when you put them together. The magnets will pull toward each other.

1. ✓ Checkpoint When do magnets repel each other?

2. Art in Science Draw a picture of how you can use a magnet. Label your picture.

What a Magnet Can Attract

You have learned that magnets attract some metal objects. Magnets will not attract all metal objects. A magnet will attract a nail. Some nails are made of iron. A magnet will not attract a penny. A penny is made of copper. Iron and copper are two kinds of metal.

You can use a magnet to find out which kinds of metal objects it will attract. Which objects in the picture do you think a magnet will attract?

Magnets do not attract marbles or a toothbrush.

A magnet can move some things without even touching them. Look at the picture below. The force of the magnet moves this train.

✓ **Lesson Checkpoint**

1. What is one kind of metal a magnet will attract?

2. **Writing** in Science Make a list in your **science journal.** What are some objects a magnet will attract?

Investigate What can magnets do?

Materials

2 magnets

small objects

paper clip

plastic cup

cup with water

paper square

What to Do

1 Push the magnets together. What happens each time?

2 Predict which objects a magnet will pull. Try to pull each object.

Process Skills

When you **interpret data**, you use your chart to answer a question.

3 Try to pull a paper clip through things.
Record what you **observe**.

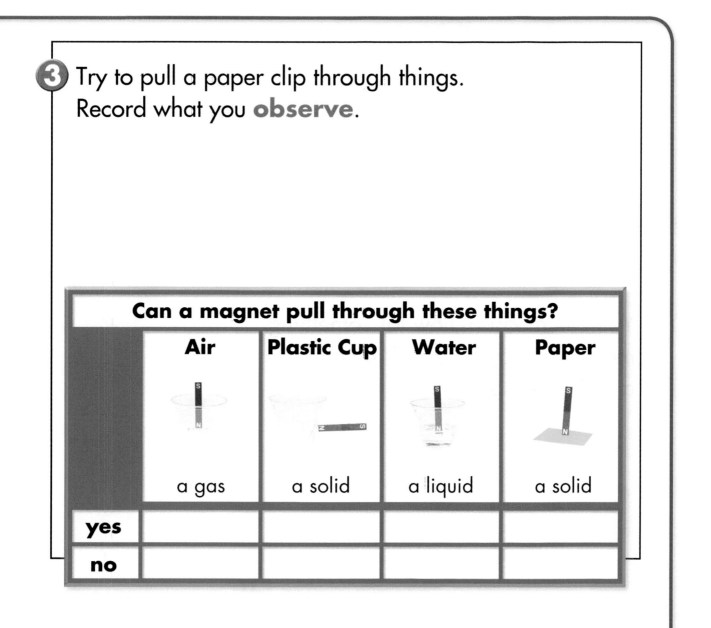

Can a magnet pull through these things?				
	Air a gas	**Plastic Cup** a solid	**Water** a liquid	**Paper** a solid
yes				
no				

Explain Your Results

1. What objects did you predict a magnet would pull? Which objects did it pull?

2. **Interpret Data** What things could the magnet pull through?

Go Further

Can magnets pull objects through a piece of foil? Make a plan to find out.

Math in Science

Measuring Motion

You can measure how far something moves. The toy truck will roll farther with a higher ramp.

50 cm

30 cm

1. How far did the toy truck roll after going down the low ramp?

2. How far did the toy truck roll after going down the high ramp?

3. How much farther did the truck roll after going down the high ramp? Write a number sentence.

Lab zone Take-Home Activity

Look for places in your neighborhood that use ramps to help people. Talk with your family about the ways that ramps can help us.

Vocabulary

Which picture goes with each word?

1. force

2. motion

3. simple machine

4. attract

5. repel

What did you learn?

6. Name two ways that objects can move.

7. What two things do you need for work to be done?

8. How does friction slow down a soccer ball on a grassy surface?

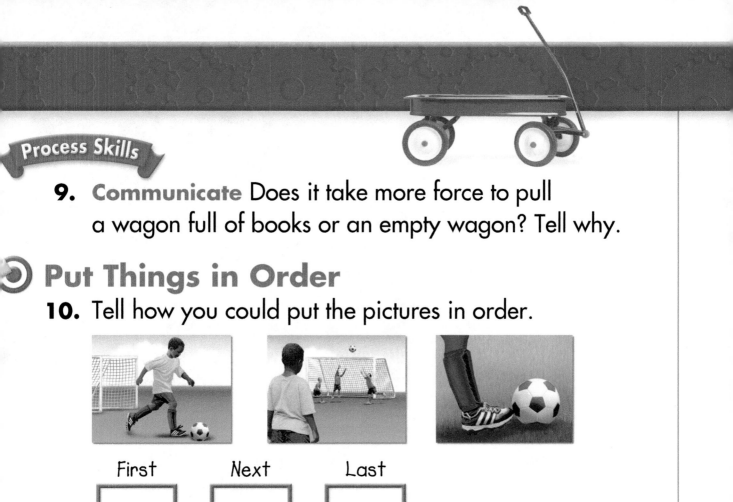

9. Communicate Does it take more force to pull a wagon full of books or an empty wagon? Tell why.

Put Things in Order

10. Tell how you could put the pictures in order.

First   Next   Last

⬜ → ⬜ → ⬜

Test Prep

Fill in the circle next to the correct answer.

11. Which can be used as a lever?

Ⓐ a wagon
Ⓑ a slide
Ⓒ a screwdriver
Ⓓ a ramp

12. **Writing** in Science Write a sentence. Tell how you can make your friends move faster on a playground merry-go-round.

Meet
Luther Jenkins

Read Together

Luther Jenkins works at NASA. He is an Aerospace Engineer. He studies airplanes.

Math and science were Luther's favorite subjects in school. At first, Luther wanted to become a lawyer. He soon discovered that he liked to learn how things work. He decided to become an engineer.

At NASA, Luther uses math and science in his work. He uses wind tunnels to conduct experiments on airplanes. He works with special lasers to measure the speed of air.

Lab zone Take-Home Activity

Use the Internet or an encyclopedia to learn about the airplane flown by the Wright brothers in 1903. Draw a picture of their airplane.

You Will Discover

- how sounds can be different.
- how sound travels.

Chapter 11

Sound

online
Student Edition
pearsonsuccessnet.com

How is sound made?

vibrate

loudness

330

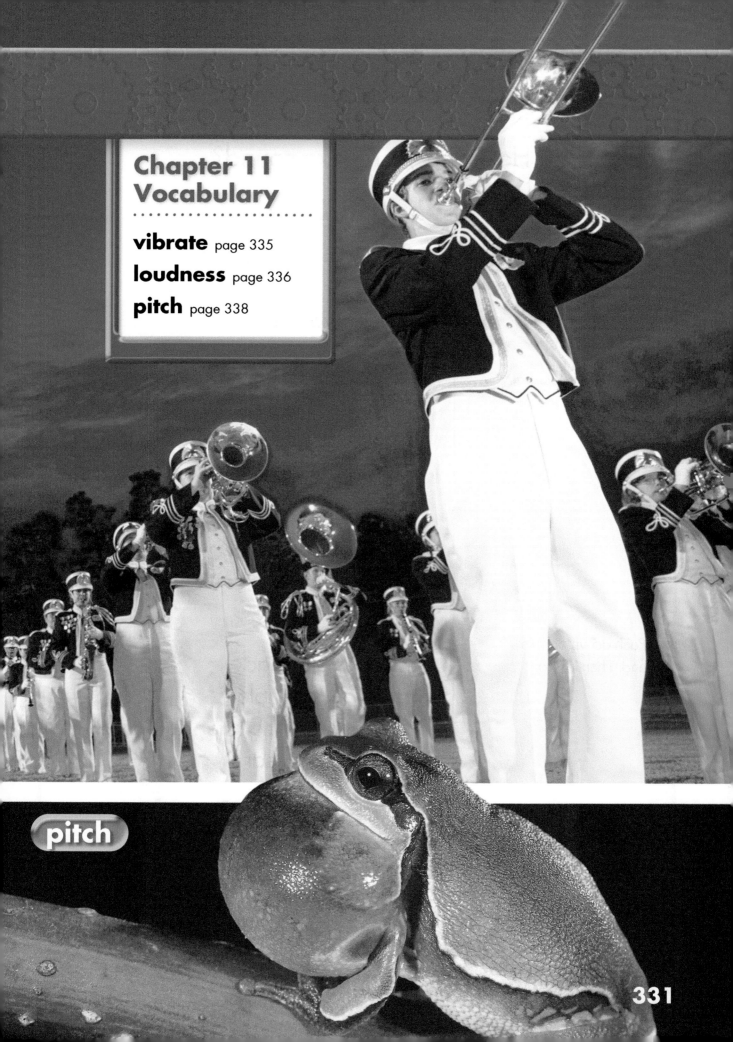

Chapter 11 Vocabulary

vibrate page 335

loudness page 336

pitch page 338

pitch

Explore How can you make sound?

Materials

safety goggles

ruler

What to Do

1 Push down on one end of the ruler. Let go. **Observe**. What do you hear?

Hold this end down.

Push down on this end. Then let go.

2 Slide the ruler back farther on the table. Push down on the ruler again. What do you hear?

Explain Your Results

Observe Think about what your heard. How did the sound change when you moved the ruler back?

Reading Skills

TARGET SKILL
Important Details

Important details are the words that tell you what you need to know.

Science Article

Sounds

Instruments can make soft sounds or loud sounds. Some instruments that make loud sounds are drums, cymbals, and tubas. Some instruments that make soft sounds are flutes, violins, and triangles.

Apply It!

Observe Read the article and look at the picture. What are some instruments that make soft sounds?

flute — Instruments that make soft sounds

🎵 Listen to the Sounds!

Sung to the tune of "Sidewalks of New York"
Lyrics by Gerri Brioso & Richard Freitas/The Dovetail Group, Inc.

Soft sounds, loud sounds,
High sounds and some low.
Listen for sounds all around you
Everywhere that you may go.

Lesson 1

What is sound?

There are many different instruments in a marching band. Each instrument makes a different sound when it is played.

How is sound made? Sound is made when an object vibrates. **Vibrate** means to move quickly back and forth. The instruments make the air vibrate to make sounds.

Loudness

One way to describe sound is by its loudness. **Loudness** means how loud or soft a sound is.

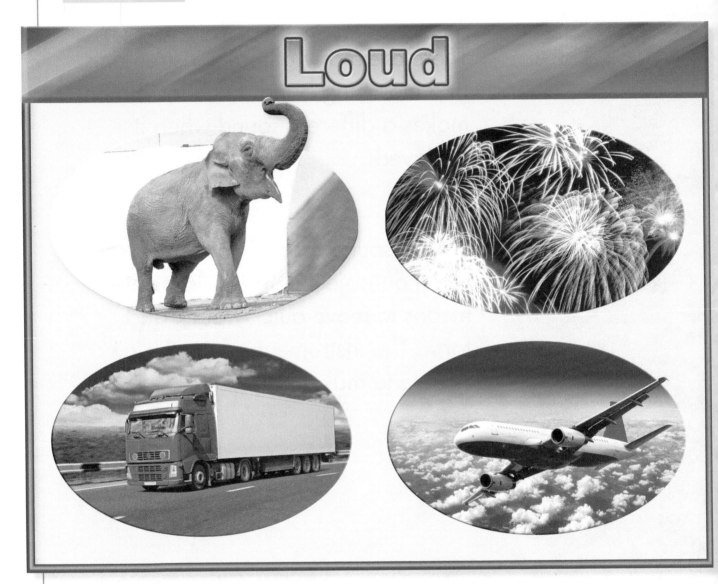

Loud

Suppose you hit a drum very hard. You would make a loud sound. The pictures on this page show things that can make loud sounds.

Suppose you lightly tapped a drum. You would make a soft sound. The pictures on this page show things that can make soft sounds.

Soft

✔ **Lesson Checkpoint**

1. What does *loudness* mean?
2. **Writing** in Science Think of one soft sound and one loud sound. Write two sentences in your **science journal** to explain how these sounds are different.

Lesson 2

What is pitch?

Pitch is another way to describe sound. **Pitch** means how high or low a sound is. Objects that vibrate quickly make a sound with a high pitch. Objects that vibrate slowly make a sound with a low pitch.

The air inside a bottle vibrates when you blow air across the bottle. Bottles with a lot of air make sounds with a low pitch. Bottles with less air make sounds with a higher pitch.

✓ Lesson Checkpoint

1. What does *pitch* mean?
2. 🔵 **Important Details** How does the way objects vibrate change pitch?

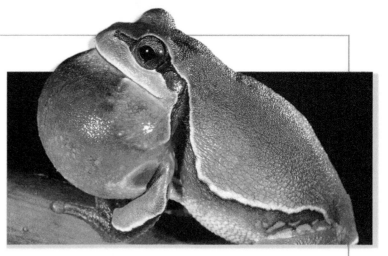

The bird makes sounds that have a high pitch. The bullfrog makes sounds that have a low pitch.

Which bottle makes the sound with the highest pitch?

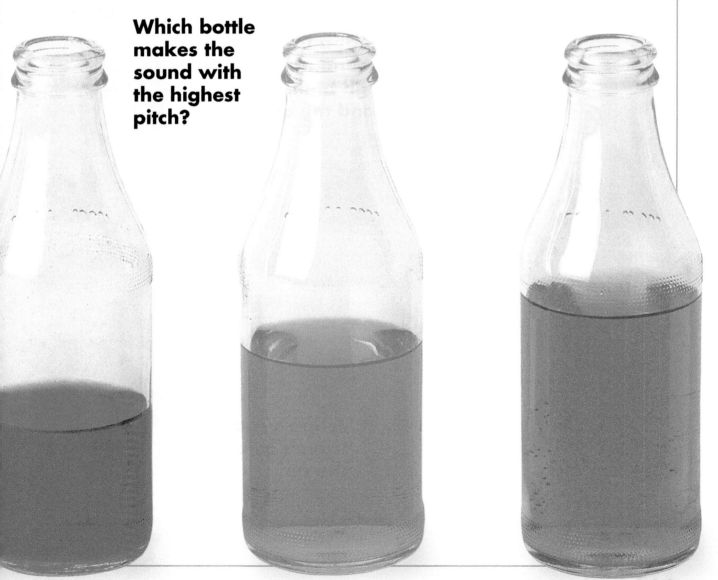

How does sound travel?

Sound travels through solids, liquids, and gases. Sound travels through gases such as air.

A woodpecker pecks at a tree. The sound moves through both the tree and the air.

A lion's roar travels through the air.

Sound travels faster through liquids, such as water, than it does through air. Sound travels fastest through solids such as wood or metal.

Dolphins whistle and click. Their sounds move through water.

1. Does sound travel faster through air or water?

2. Art in Science Draw a picture of an animal that is making a sound. Write a sentence that tells about the sound.

Lesson 4

How do some animals make sounds?

Animals make sounds in many ways. The pictures show some ways animals use parts of their bodies to make sounds.

wings

A cricket makes sounds by rubbing one wing on the other wing. Then the other wing vibrates to make sound. The sound is like running your finger across the teeth of a comb.

342

A rattlesnake makes sounds like maracas. The snake shakes the rattle in its tail.

A spiny lobster makes sounds like a violin. The violin is played by rubbing the bow against the strings. The lobster uses its antenna like a bow. It rubs its antenna along the side of its head.

antenna

✓ **Lesson Checkpoint**

1. What instrument does a spiny lobster sound like?

2. 🎯 **Important Details** How does a cricket make sounds?

Lesson 5

What are some sounds around you?

Listen closely to the sounds around you. You might hear a siren or a group of children laughing. You might hear a fly buzz as it goes by. We hear many different sounds every day. Look at the picture. What sounds might the people and the objects in the picture make?

1. ✓ **Checkpoint** What kinds of sounds do you hear in your neighborhood?

2. **Writing** in Science Write one or two sentences in your **science journal.** Tell what sounds you might hear at your school.

Investigate How can you change sound?

Materials

safety goggles

rubber band

tissue box

2 pencils

What to Do

1 Put the rubber band around the box. Put 2 pencils under the rubber band.

2 Pluck the rubber band hard. Then pluck gently.

Wear your safety goggles.

3 Fill in the chart. **Infer**. What changes the sound?

	Is the sound loud or soft?
Hard plucks	
Gentle plucks	

Process Skills

When you **predict**, you tell what you think will happen.

4 Pluck the rubber band again. Move the pencils farther apart. **Predict** whether the sound will be higher or lower. Pluck the rubber band again.

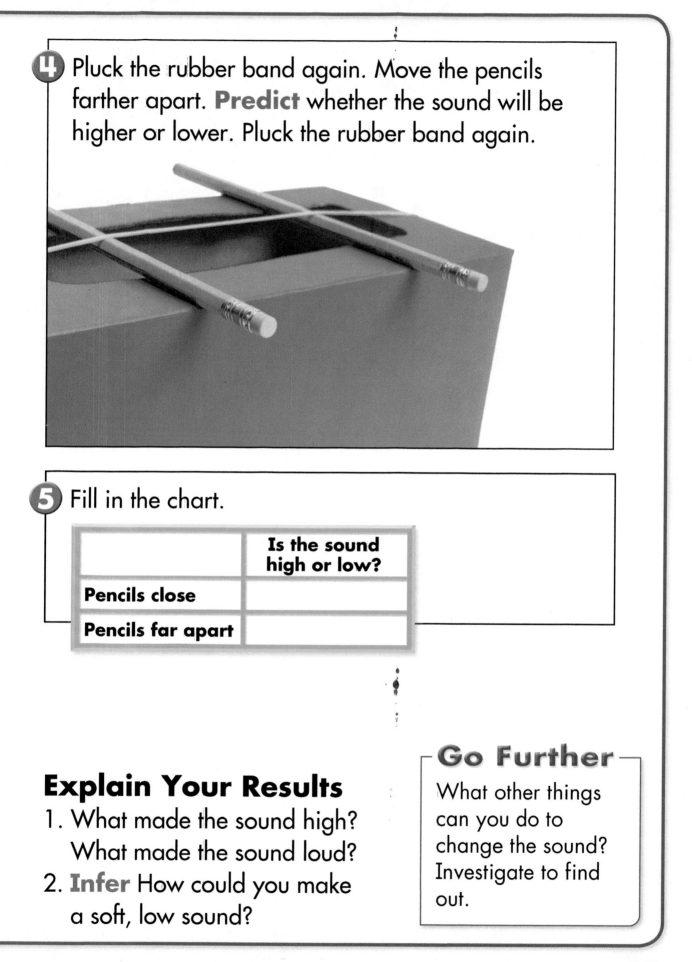

5 Fill in the chart.

	Is the sound high or low?
Pencils close	
Pencils far apart	

Explain Your Results

1. What made the sound high? What made the sound loud?
2. **Infer** How could you make a soft, low sound?

Go Further
What other things can you do to change the sound? Investigate to find out.

Math in Science

Measuring Sounds

This bar graph compares the loudness of some sounds. A vacuum cleaner is much louder than a whisper.

Loudness of Sounds

Units of Loudness

160
150
140
130
120
110
100
90
80
70
60
50
40
30
20
10
0

Whisper   Talk   Vacuum Cleaner   Band Concert   Jet Plane

Kinds of Sound

Use the graph to answer each question.

1. What is the softest sound in the graph? How many units of sound does it have?

2. What is the loudest sound in the graph? How many units of sound does it have?

3. How many more units of sound does talking have than whispering?

Lab zone **Take-Home Activity**

Hit pots and pans gently with a spoon. Which ones have a high pitch? Which ones have a low pitch? Put them in order from lowest to highest pitch.

Vocabulary
Which picture goes with each word?

1. pitch
2. vibrate

A

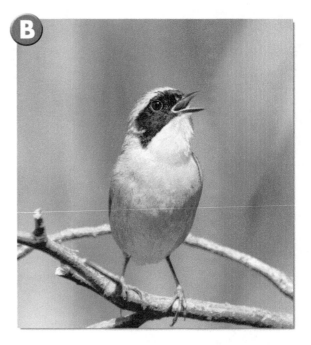

B

. . . .

What did you learn?

3. What word describes how loud or soft a sound is?

4. What does *vibrate* mean?

5. Does sound travel fastest through solids, liquids, or gases?

6. Observe Think about lunch time at your school. What sounds might you hear?

Important Details

7. What are some words you can use to describe sound?

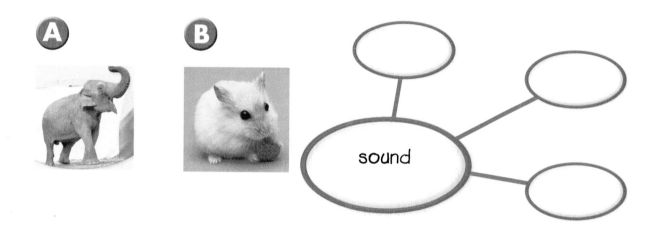

A

B

sound

Test Prep

Fill in the circle next to the correct answer.

8. Which is made when an object vibrates quickly?

Ⓐ low pitch sound
Ⓑ high pitch sound
Ⓒ soft sound
Ⓓ loud sound

9. Writing in Science Choose an animal. Tell about how that animal makes sounds.

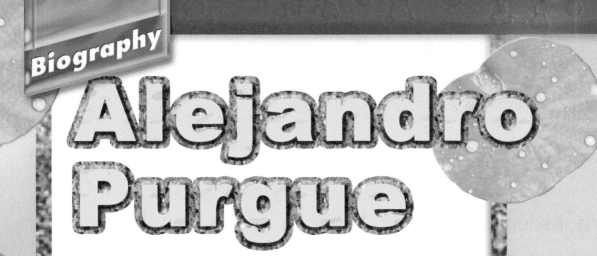

Alejandro Purgue

Read Together

Alejandro Purgue studies animals and the sounds they make. People and many animals make sounds using vocal chords in their throats.

While Dr. Purgue was studying bullfrogs, he made an amazing discovery. Bullfrogs actually make most of their sound through their ears!

Like other animals, bullfrogs also use their ears for hearing. Think about this amazing fact the next time you hear a frog ribbit!

Lab zone Take-Home Activity

Go outside at home and listen to the sounds around you. Make a list of the sounds you hear. Write *quiet* or *loud* next to each sound.

Unit C Test Talk

Test-Taking
Strategies

Find Important Words
▷ Choose the Right Answer
Use Information from
Text and Graphics
Write Your Answer

Choose the Right Answer

Remove wrong answer choices to
help you choose the right answer.

Lunch

Emil made himself lunch.
He used bread, peanut
butter, and jelly to make
a sandwich. Emil poured
juice to drink.

Which state of matter is juice?

Ⓐ bread
Ⓑ solid
Ⓒ liquid
Ⓓ jelly

Your answer should be a state of matter.
Find the two answers that are states of matter.
Which one answers the question?

Unit C Wrap-Up

Chapter 8

What are some properties of matter?
- Some properties of matter are color, shape, and size. Mass and how it feels are also properties of matter.

Chapter 9

What are some kinds of energy?
- Solar energy, light, and electricity are some kinds of energy.

Chapter 10

How do forces cause objects to move?
- The amount of force used on an object affects how far and how fast the object moves.

Chapter 11

How is sound made?
- Sound is made when an abject vibrates.
- Loudness is how loud or soft a sound is.
- Pitch is how high or low a sound is.

Performance Assessment

Make a Musical Instrument

- Use solids, liquids, or gases to make sounds.
- Play a song for your class.
- Ask your class to name the solids, liquids, and gases you used to make the sounds.

Read More About Physical Science!

Look for books like these in your library.

Full Inquiry

Experiment What kinds of objects reflect light clearly?

Some objects reflect light. Others do not. Find out what kinds of objects reflect light clearly.

Materials

mirror and flashlight

construction paper and paper with wrinkles

foil with wrinkles

white paper

Ask a question.
What kinds of objects reflect light clearly?

Make your hypothesis.
Do smooth and shiny objects reflect light as clearly as other objects? Tell what you think.

Plan a fair test.
Make sure the objects are the same size. Use the same flashlight.

Do your test.

1 **Observe** the mirror. Is it smooth? Is it shiny? Record in the chart.

2 Shine light on the mirror. Observe. Does the mirror reflect light clearly?

3 Test the other objects.
Record. Do steps 1
and 2 again.

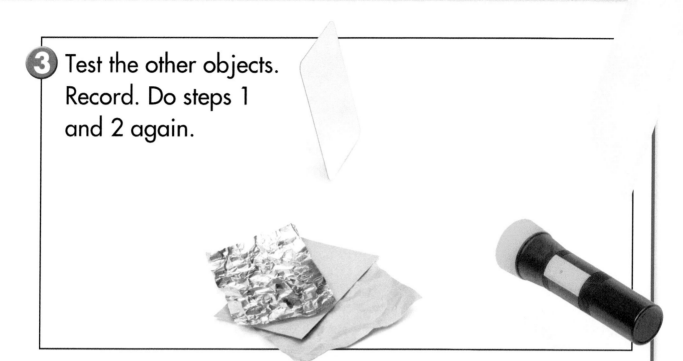

Collect and record data.

	Is it smooth? yes or no	**Is it shiny?** yes or no	**Does it reflect light clearly?** yes or no

Tell Your Conclusion.

Do smooth and shiny objects
reflect light clearly? How do
you know?

Go Further
What might happen
if you test other
classroom objects?
Experiment to find
out.

Icicles

The water falls quick, quick in drips,
One bright winter afternoon.
As night comes on, the temperature dips,
And then you'll see quite soon

The dripping slows and ice appears,
Long icicles have formed.
The spikes of ice, like glassy tears,
Won't drip until they're warmed.

Icicles don't stay for long,
Once the sun's rays come out strong.

Science Fair Projects

Using Scientific Methods
1. Ask a question.
2. Make a hypothesis.
3. Plan a fair test.
4. Do your test.
5. Collect and record data.
6. Tell your conclusions.
7. Go further.

Idea 1
Energy in My Terrarium

Plan a project. Find out how different amounts of sunlight affect how plants grow and change.

Idea 2
Listening to Sound Through Matter

Plan a project. Find out how loudness changes when you listen to sounds through different types of matter.

Unit D

Space and Technology

Unit D

Chapter 12 Earth and Space

Directed Inquiry	What causes day and night?
Guided Inquiry	How can you make a model of a constellation?
Activity Flip Chart	What causes the seasons? What do constellations look like?
Quick Activity Transparencies	What is the Sun like? How does Earth spin? What are the seasons? What do you see in the night sky? Why does the Moon change? What is the solar system?

Chapter 13 Technology in Our World

Directed Inquiry	How can you move the ball?
Guided Inquiry	How can you make a maze?
Activity Flip Chart	How can you make a model of a helicopter? How can you build a strong bridge?
Quick Activity Transparencies	What is technology? How does technology help people? How can technology help people communicate? What are some ways technology helps people? What are some things that people make?

Unit D

Full Inquiry	Which tissue is the strongest?

You Will Discover

- what is in the day and night sky.
- how Earth, the Sun, and the Moon move.

Chapter 12
Earth and Space

online
Student Edition
pearsonsuccessnet.com

What are some ways the Earth moves?

solar system

rotation axis

constellation

362

orbit

Chapter 12 Vocabulary

axis page 370

rotation page 370

orbit page 374

constellation page 376

crater page 378

phase page 381

solar system page 382

crater

phase

Explore What causes day and night?

Materials

foam ball

pencil

dot sticker

crayons or markers

flashlight

What to Do

① **Make a model** of Earth.

foam ball

red dot sticker

child

② Shine a flashlight on your model.

The flashlight is like the Sun.

③ Turn your model of Earth. Watch the child.

Explain Your Results

How does your **model** show day and night?

How to Read Science

Reading Skills

TARGET SKILL

Alike and Different

Alike means how things are the same.
Different means how things are not the same.

Science Pictures

Day and Night

Apply It!
Look at the pictures.
Tell how day and night
are alike and different.
Think of your **model**
to help you.

Alike	Different

365

You Are There

The Sun

Sung to the tune of "Twinkle Twinkle Little Star"
Lyrics by Gerri Brioso & Richard Freitas/The Dovetail Group, Inc.

In the sky's a great big star.
It's the Sun and it's real far!
The Sun lights up the sky so bright.
It also lights the Moon at night.
Heat and light come from the Sun
And that is needed by everyone!

Lesson 1
What is the Sun?

Think of the stars you see in the sky at night. Stars are made of hot, glowing gases. The Sun is a star too. The Sun seems brighter and larger than the other stars. This is because the Sun is the closest star to Earth. The Sun is so bright that you cannot see other stars during the day.

Why We Need the Sun

The Sun may look small, but it is really very big. The Sun is much bigger than Earth. The Sun looks small because it is so far away.

This is what the Sun looks like in space.

The Sun is important to Earth. Earth gets light and heat from the Sun. Living things on Earth need light and heat. People, plants, and animals can live on Earth because of the Sun.

✓ Lesson Checkpoint

1. Why is the Sun important to living things on Earth?

2. 🎯 How are the Sun and other stars **alike** and **different?**

What causes day and night?

The picture shows an imaginary line through the center of Earth. This line is called an **axis.** Earth is always spinning on its axis. This spinning on an axis is called a **rotation.** Earth makes one complete rotation each day.

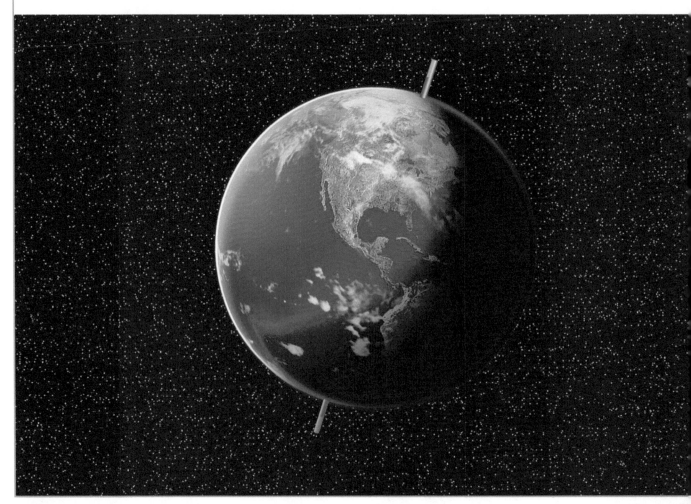

Earth's rotation causes day and night.
When your side of Earth is facing the Sun,
you have day. When your side of Earth
is facing away from the Sun, you have night.

✓ Checkpoint

1. What is Earth's axis?

2. **Writing in Science** Write 2 sentences
in your **science journal.** Tell why one
side of Earth has day when the other
side has night.

**It takes about
24 hours for
Earth to make
one complete
rotation.**

The Sun in the Sky

The Sun seems to move across the sky during the day. The Sun looks low in the sky early in the morning. By the middle of the day, the Sun is high in the sky. In the evening, the Sun is low in the sky again.

sunrise

noon

The Sun is always shining. The Sun is hard to see on some days.

The Sun is not really moving across the
sky. The Sun only looks like it is moving.
It is really the Earth that is moving.

sunset

✓ Lesson Checkpoint

1. Why does the Sun look like it is moving
   across the sky?

2. **Writing** in Science   Write 2 sentences in your
   science journal. Tell what time sunrise and
   sunset are today where you live.

Lesson 3

What causes seasons to change?

Earth is tilted on its axis. Earth is always tilted in the same direction.

You know that Earth spins on its axis. Earth moves around the Sun in an orbit too. An **orbit** is a path around another object.

It takes Earth about one year to orbit the Sun one time. The tilt of Earth and its orbit cause the seasons.

✓ Lesson Checkpoint

1. What causes the seasons?

2. **Social Studies** in Science Look at a calendar. When is the official first day of summer?

summer

In summer, the part of Earth where we live is tilted toward the Sun.

In spring, the part of the Earth where we live is beginning to tilt toward the Sun.

In winter, the part of Earth where we live is tilted away from the Sun.

In fall, the part of Earth where we live is beginning to tilt away from the Sun.

Lesson 4

What can you see in the night sky?

You can see many other stars at night. Stars in the night sky look small because they are far away. Sometimes it looks like there are more stars than you can count!

Long ago, people thought they saw patterns in some groups of stars. They imagined lines that formed pictures. A group of stars that form a picture is called a **constellation.**

This constellation looks like a lion. It is called Leo.

1. ✓Checkpoint What is a constellation?

2. Technology in Science What tools can you use to see the stars better at night?

Look at these two constellations. They are called the Big Dipper and the Little Dipper.

The Moon

You might see the Moon in the night sky too. The Moon is the largest and brightest object in the night sky.

The Moon has mountains and deep craters. A **crater** is a hole in the ground that is shaped like a bowl. A crater is formed when a large rock from space hits the Moon.

The Moon has many craters like this one.

Sometimes you can see the Moon in the daytime.

1. What causes craters on the Moon?

2. **Art** in Science Draw a picture of the clear night sky. Use chalk and dark paper.

Lesson 5

Why does the Moon seem to change?

The Moon rotates just like Earth. It moves in an orbit around Earth. The Moon orbits Earth while Earth orbits the Sun. It takes about four weeks for the Moon to orbit Earth one time.

phases of the moon

The Moon does not make its own light. The Moon reflects light from the Sun. You only see the part of the Moon that has light shining on it.

The Moon seems to change shape. Sometimes the Moon looks round. Sometimes you see smaller parts of the Moon. Sometimes you cannot see the Moon at all. The shape of the lighted part of the Moon is called a **phase.**

The Moon is the biggest and brightest object in the night sky.

✓ **Lesson Checkpoint**

1. Why can we see the Moon?

2. **Math** in Science How long will it take for the Moon to move around the Earth 3 times?

What is the solar system?

Earth is a planet. You know that Earth orbits around the Sun. Other planets orbit around the Sun too. The planets and their moons and other objects that move around the Sun are called the **solar system.**

Sun

Mercury

Venus

Earth

Mars

Jupiter

The Sun is the center of our solar system.
All of the objects in the solar system orbit the
Sun. Count the other planets that orbit the
Sun. How many planets do you count?

✓ **Lesson Checkpoint**

1. What is at the center of Earth's solar system?

2. 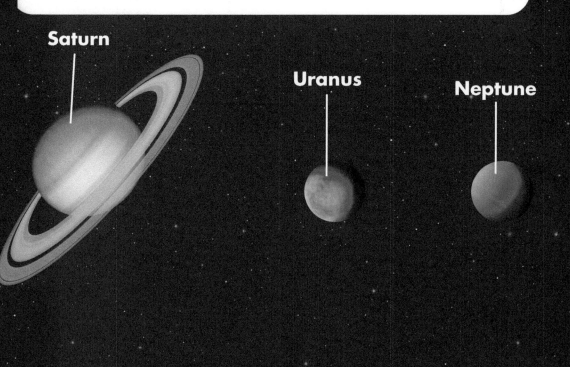 Look at the planets. Tell how they are **alike** and **different**.

Saturn

Uranus

Neptune

Investigate How can you make a model of a constellation?

Materials

safety goggles

pencil

black paper

flashlight

What to Do

1 Make a **model** constellation. Poke holes through the paper with a pencil.

2 Make the room dark. Hold the paper near a wall.

Process Skills

You use what you learn to **make a definition** of a constellation.

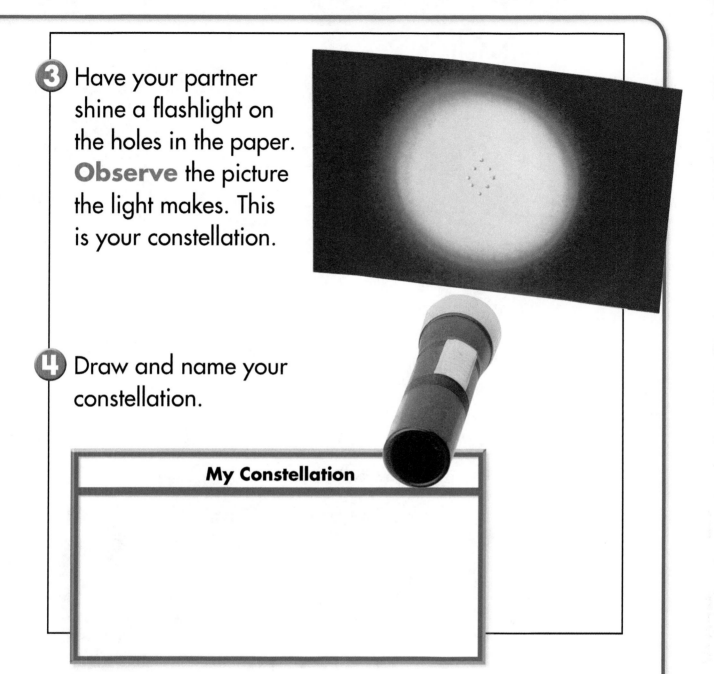

3 Have your partner shine a flashlight on the holes in the paper. **Observe** the picture the light makes. This is your constellation.

4 Draw and name your constellation.

My Constellation

Explain Your Results

1. Tell about your constellation. How is your model like a real constellation? How is it different?

2. **Make a definition** of a constellation.

Go Further

How else could you make a model of your constellation? Investigate to find out.

Planets in Orbit

Each planet takes a different number of days to orbit the Sun. This table shows how long the orbits are for some of the planets.

Mercury Venus Earth Mars

Jupiter

Planet	Orbit
Earth	365 days
Mercury	88 days
Venus	225 days
Mars	687 days

1. Which of these planets takes the most number of days to orbit the Sun?

2. Which of these planets takes the fewest number of days to orbit the Sun?

3. List these planets in order from the fewest to the most number of days to orbit the Sun.

Uranus

Neptune

Saturn

Lab zone Take-Home Activity

Work with your family to find out how many days it takes each of the planets to orbit the Sun. Use the Internet and other resources to help you.

Vocabulary

Which picture goes with each word?

1. axis
2. crater
3. constellation
4. orbit
5. phase
6. rotation
7. solar system

What did you learn?

8. What is caused by Earth's rotation?

9. Why is the Sun the only star you can see during the day?

10. Communicate Tell why we have light during the day.

Alike and Different

11. Tell how the Sun and the Moon are **alike** and **different**.

Alike	Different

Test Prep

Fill in the circle next to the correct answer.

12. Which star is closest to Earth?

Ⓐ the Sun

Ⓑ the Big Dipper

Ⓒ the Moon

Ⓓ Leo

13. Writing in Science Describe what you might see if you traveled around the solar system.

Mission To Mars

NASA scientists want to learn more about the planet Mars. Mars is a planet that is close to Earth. Mars and Earth are alike in some ways. Water is needed for life on Earth. Scientists want to learn more about water on Mars.

NASA sent robots to Mars to learn about the planet. Some robots fly around Mars taking pictures. Some robots called rovers have landed on Mars. These rovers travel across the surface.

Scientists use the robots to study the environment on Mars. They take pictures of the soil and the rocks on Mars. Rovers also dig into the ground.

This rover is called *Opportunity*. *Opportunity* landed in a place called Meridiani Planum.

Lab zone Take-Home Activity

Suppose you are a scientist studying Mars. Write a question that you have about Mars.

Astronomer

Laura Peticolas is an astronomer who works with NASA. She studies natural displays of light called *auroras*. Two examples of auroras are Northern lights and Southern lights.

Read Together

Have you ever looked at the stars at night? People who study the Sun, stars, planets, and other things far from Earth are called astronomers.

Many astronomers use special tools called telescopes to help them see far out into space. A telescope helps things that are far away look nearer, larger, and brighter.

To study the universe, scientists at NASA launch many telescopes. One such telescope is the Hubble Space Telescope. Every day this telescope sends information to astronomers all over the world.

Lab zone Take-Home Activity

Go outside on a clear night with your family. Look at the sky. Write about what you see.

Chapter 13

You Will Discover

- how technology has changed the world we live in.
- ways we use technology every day.

Technology in Our World

online
Student Edition
pearsonsuccessnet.com

technology

engine

satellite

vaccine

394

invent

Chapter 13 Vocabulary

. . . .

technology
page 399

invent page 399

transportation
page 400

engine page 400

vaccine page 402

meteorologist
page 407

satellite page 407

manufacture
page 408

transportation

manufacture

To make by hand or machine.

meteorolo

Explore How can you move the ball?

Materials

metal ball

books

cup

pencil

ruler

magnet

spoon

What to Do

1 Put the ball on the books. Place the cup 25 cm away from the books.

2 Solve this problem. Put the ball in the cup. Use tools.

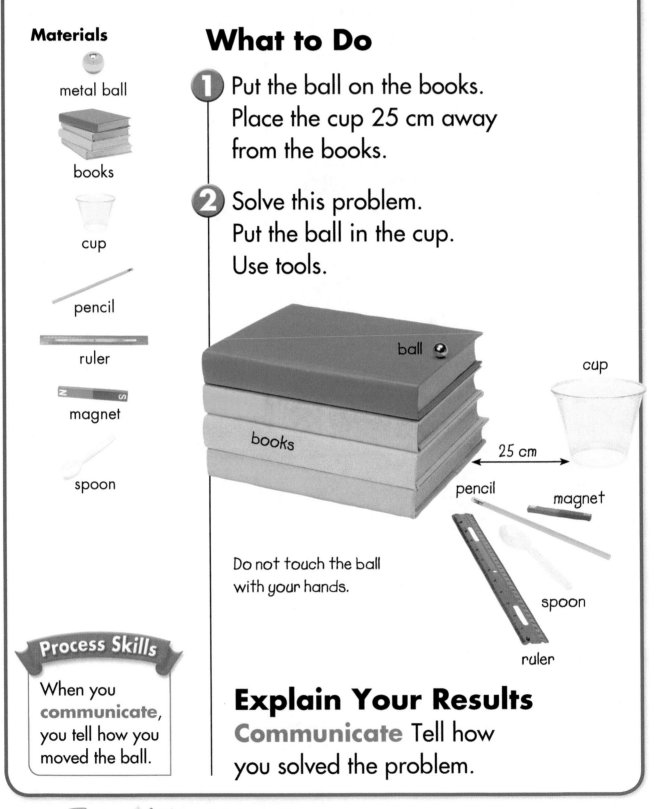

ball

cup

books

25 cm

pencil

magnet

spoon

ruler

Do not touch the ball with your hands.

Explain Your Results

Communicate Tell how you solved the problem.

How to Read Science

Reading Skills

TARGET SKILL
Retell

Retell means to tell what you learned in your own words.

Science Article

Bicycles

The first bicycle was invented in 1817. Riders pushed their feet on the ground to make it move. Pedals were added in 1839. The pedals helped people ride bicycles with their feet off the ground.

Apply It!
Communicate
Tell what you learned about bicycles.

Retell

Technology Helps Us All

Sung to the tune of "Bingo"
Lyrics by Gerri Brioso & Richard Freitas/The Dovetail Group, Inc.

Technology now helps us all
In lots of different ways. It
Helps us travel fast,
Helps us travel far,
Helps us travel safe,
In cars, and trains and airplanes.

Lesson 1

What is technology?

People ride in cars. People use computers. We can do these things because of technology. **Technology** means using science to help us solve problems.

Sometimes people use technology to invent things. **Invent** means to make something for the first time.

Inventions can be things we need or things we want. Many people need cars to travel long distances. Some people want computer games.

Changes in Transportation

Technology has changed transportation. **Transportation** moves people and things from place to place. Today people travel farther and faster than they did long ago.

Some kinds of transportation have engines. An **engine** is a machine that does work or makes something move. Long ago, steam engines made trains and boats move. Today, cars, trains, and boats have gasoline or electric engines.

Technology helps people travel. Seat belts and air bags help make cars safe. Airplanes fly faster than ever before.

People use technology to help solve problems. Gasoline can cause pollution. New cars have been invented that use gasoline and electricity. These cars help reduce pollution.

✔ **Lesson Checkpoint**

1. How has technology changed transportation?

2. **Writing** in Science Write a sentence in your **science journal.** Tell about some inventions that can help you.

Lesson 2

How does technology help us?

Technology can help people stay healthy. People use technology to make vaccines. A **vaccine** is a medicine that can help prevent a disease.

vaccine

Doctors use technology to help people. Glasses and contact lenses can help people to see. Hearing aids can help people to hear. Artificial legs can help some people to walk.

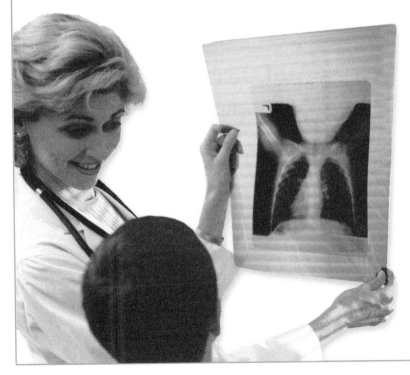

The doctor uses an x ray to help this boy get well.

This is a picture from an MRI.

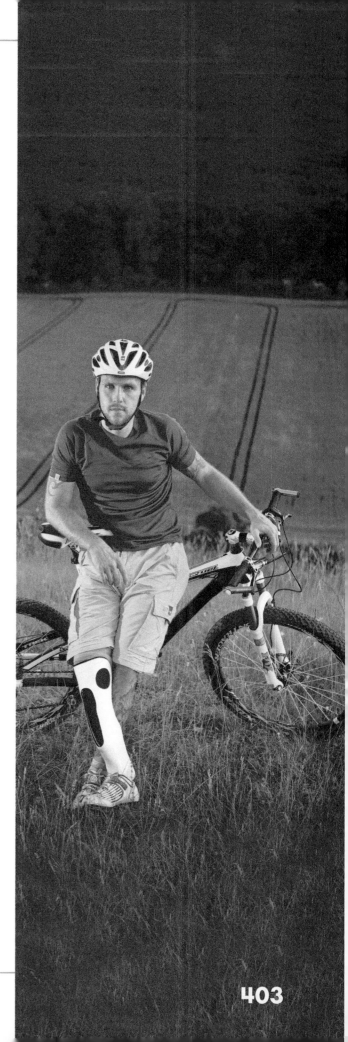

Technology can help doctors find out why people are sick. X rays, CAT scans, and MRIs are tools doctors can use to see inside people. When doctors know what is wrong, they can help people to get well.

This man can bike with the help of his artificial leg.

√ Lesson Checkpoint

1. What are some ways that technology can help people?

2. 🔄 **Retell** What are some tools that help doctors see inside people?

How do we use technology to communicate?

What are some ways you communicate with your friends? The way technology is used to communicate has changed over the years.

Long ago, telephones were attached to a wall. Today you can carry a telephone with you. Telephones are much smaller today than they were years ago.

This telephone is from 1879!

The first computers were very big and very heavy. Today, computers are smaller, faster, and easier to use than the first computers.

The first computer was invented in 1946. It filled a whole room!

✓ **Lesson Checkpoint**

1. How has technology changed the way people communicate?

2. **Math** in Science Some early telephones were about 46 centimeters tall. Today, some phones are about 9 centimeters tall. How much taller were older telephones than newer telephones?

Lesson 4

What are some other ways we use technology?

Technology has changed the way people have fun. People listen to music on compact discs. People use computers to play games.

Technology can also make our lives easier. People use Velcro® to close things. People use calculators to do math.

MP3 players play music.

Electricity can control the loudness of some guitars.

Technology helps people in their jobs. A **meteorologist** is a person who studies weather. Meteorologists study pictures taken by satellites to predict weather. A **satellite** is an object that revolves around another object.

Satellites send information about the weather to Earth.

Meteorologists get information about the weather from satellites.

✔ Lesson Checkpoint

1. How does a meteorologist use information from satellites?

2. **Writing** in Science Write a sentence in your **science journal.** Tell three ways you used technology today.

How do people make things?

People manufacture things we use every day. **Manufacture** means to make by hand or by machines. Coats and bicycles are two things that are manufactured.

Natural materials were used to make parts of this coat.

Different types of materials are used to manufacture things. Some materials come from nature. This coat was made using wool from sheep. The buttons were made from wood.

Some materials are made by people.
The seat of this bicycle is made from plastic.
The tires are made from rubber. Plastic and
rubber are materials made by people.

**This bike uses
materials made
by people.**

✓ **Lesson Checkpoint**

1. What are some manufactured things you
use in school?

2. 🔄 **Retell** What are some materials
used to make a bicycle?

Investigate How can you make a maze?

Materials

safety goggles

marble

cardboard

paper tubes

box

tape and scissors

What to Do

1. How can you make a maze that a marble can follow? Make a plan. Draw it.

2. Tape paper tubes to the cardboard.

3. **Predict** Will your maze work?

4. Test your maze. **Observe** the marble. Move the tubes to make the maze work better.

Process Skills

You **predict** when you tell what you think will happen.

More Lab zone Activities Take It to the Net
pearsonsuccessnet.com

5 Test your maze 2 more times.

Test your maze.	
Test	**Did the marble follow the maze?**
1	
2	
3	

Your maze might look like this one.

Be careful!

Be sure to wear your safety goggles.

Explain Your Results

Communicate Tell how the parts of your maze work together.

Go Further

How can you make your marble move in a different way? Investigate to find out.

Technology in Your School

Look around your school. How many things can you find that help people communicate? How many things can you find that help people move from place to place? Fill in your table with examples.

Technology in My School

Communication	Transportation

1. Count the examples you found for each column.
2. Compare the number of examples you found. Use <, >, or =.

Take-Home Activity

Walk around your home. Look for ways you use technology. Make a table like the one you made for your school.

Vocabulary

Which picture goes with each word?

1. engine
2. vaccine
3. satellite
4. meteorologist

What did you learn?

5. What is technology?

6. Name two ways you use technology every day.

7. How has technology changed communication?

8. Infer Why do people invent new things?

Retell

9. Tell what you learned about toothbrushes.

Retell

The first toothbrush was invented in China in the 1400s. The bristles were made from animal hair. The first electric toothbrush was invented in 1960. Today, bristles are made from nylon.

Test Prep

Fill in the circle next to the correct answer.

10. What is an object that travels around another object?

Ⓐ engine

Ⓑ vaccine

Ⓒ satellite

Ⓓ velcro

11. **Writing** in Science Make a list. Tell how people use technology.

Biography

Meet Shonte Wright

Shonte Wright traveled across the United States with five other scientists. They told people about the rovers that landed on Mars in 2004.

Read Together

In 2004 NASA sent two robots to Mars. The robots were called rovers. The rovers took pictures of Mars and sent them back to Earth. NASA used the pictures to study the planet.

Shonte Wright is one of the scientists who worked with NASA on the rovers. She helped make sure the rovers would still work after the long trip through space.

Ms. Wright knew she wanted to be a scientist and work at NASA when she was ten years old. She took many math and science classes to help her get ready for her job.

Lab zone Take-Home Activity

Suppose you are going to invent a robot to explore another planet. Draw what the robot would look like.

Test-Taking
Strategies

Find Important Words

Choose the Right Answer

Use Information from
Text and Graphics

▶ Write Your Answer

Write Your Answer

You can write your answer to science questions. Remember that your answer should be short but complete.

Doctors use technology to help you when you are sick or hurt. They can use X-ray, CAT scan, or an MRI to see inside your body. Best of all, using these machines doesn't hurt!

Read the question. Look at the text.

Why does a doctor use X-ray or CAT scan technology?

Which words can you use to help write your answer? Write your answer.

Unit D Wrap-Up

Chapter 12

What are some ways the Earth moves?
- Earth is always spinning on its axis.
- Earth moves around the Sun in an orbit.

Chapter 13

What are some ways technology helps us?
- Technology helps people travel, communicate, and make things.
- Doctors use technology to help people get well.

Performance Assessment

Make a Technology Collage

- Find pictures of people using technology to communicate.

- Cut out the pictures.

- Make a collage.

- Tell about the pictures you found.

Read More About Space & Technology!

Look for books like these in your library.

Starry Messenger

PETER SÍS

The PLANETS in Our SOLAR SYSTEM

by Franklyn M. Branley
illustrated by Kevin O'Malley

BY GAIL GIBBONS
THE MOON BOOK

Lab zone Full Inquiry

Experiment Which tissue is the strongest?

Tissues can be strong or weak. Experiment to find out which tissue is the strongest. The tissue that holds the most water is the strongest.

Materials

3 tissues

jar and rubber band

dropper and cup with water

marbles

balance

gram cubes

Ask a question.

Are tissues that cost more stronger than tissues that cost less?

Make a hypothesis.

If a tissue costs the most, then it is the strongest.

Plan a fair test.

Use the same amount of water to wet each tissue. Use 3 different brands of tissue.

Do your test.

1 Put a tissue on the jar. Put a rubber band around it.

2 Wet the tissue drop by drop. Use 30 drops.

3 Carefully place one marble at a time on top of the tissue.

4 Count how many marbles it takes to break the tissue.

5 **Measure** the mass of the marbles.

6 Repeat with the other tissues.

Collect and record data.

Tissue Cost	How many marbles?	How many grams?
Most		
Middle		
Least		

Tell your conclusion.
Which tissue is the strongest?

Go Further
What if you used less water to wet each tissue? Try it and find out.

Stars at Night

Bright stars in the black night sky,
Cannot help catching your eye.
The number of stars is so great,
How do people keep stars straight?

Here's a way—people long ago,
Gazed at the sky from far below.
They looked for patterns and wrote them down,
Like Little Horse and Northern Crown.

So when you see the stars above,
You might search for Great Bear and Dove.

Science Fair Projects

Full Inquiry

Using Scientific Methods
1. Ask a question.
2. Make a hypothesis.
3. Plan a fair test.
4. Do your test.
5. Collect and record data.
6. Tell your conclusion.
7. Go further.

Idea 1
Phases of the Moon

Plan a project. Find out what the Moon looks like every day for one month.

Idea 2
Flying Better

Make a plan. Find out if changing the size of a helicopter's blades will make it fly better.

Metric and Customary Measurement

Science uses the metric system to measure things. Metric measurement is used around the world. Here is how different metric measurements compare to customary measurement.

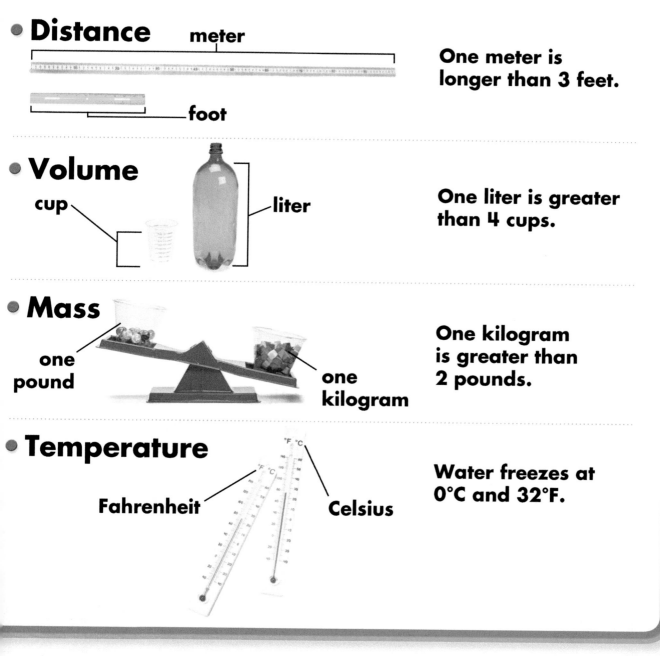

- **Distance**

  meter

  foot

  One meter is longer than 3 feet.

- **Volume**

  cup

  liter

  One liter is greater than 4 cups.

- **Mass**

  one pound

  one kilogram

  One kilogram is greater than 2 pounds.

- **Temperature**

  Fahrenheit

  Celsius

  Water freezes at 0°C and 32°F.

Compost Gold!

Rosa and Joe like to garden. Rosa grows colorful roses. Joe grows prize-winning pumpkins. They have a gardening secret — they add compost to the soil in their gardens!

What Is Compost?

Rosa and Joe read about compost in school. They learned that when plants die, they slowly break down. These dead plants transform into a dark brown material. This is compost. Compost makes the soil better for growing plants.

Every day, yard and kitchen wastes get thrown away. These wastes take up space in landfills. A landfill is a place where waste and garbage are buried. Landfills are a growing problem in many places.

Compost can help fix this problem. Instead of tossing out wastes, we can recycle wastes into compost.

What You Can Compost

Rosa and Joe discovered that many things can be put in a compost pile instead of in the garbage can.

People can make compost from such things as dead leaves, grass clippings, and twigs.

Kitchen wastes such as eggshells, nutshells, fruits, and vegetables can all be added too. Pieces of cardboard, newspapers, and paper towels can be added to the compost.

What you Can Compost

leaves   grass clippings   twigs

hay   straw   eggshells

nutshells   old fruits and vegetables

cardboard   newspapers   paper towels

What You Cannot Compost

Some wastes should *not* go into the compost pile. They should go into the garbage instead.

Meat, fish, bones, cheese, and milk should not be added to a compost pile.

What You Cannot Compost

Fish   Meat

Bones   Cheese   Milk

Rosa and Joe used what they learned to design and make their own compost bin. You can make your own mini-compost bin. Follow the directions and watch what happens!

What to Do

1. Put some food scraps, leaves, grass, and soil into the jar.
2. Write a list of the items you put in the jar.
3. Add a small amount of water. Then stir the compost with the plastic spoon. Put the lid on the jar.
4. Observe the jar each day for 2 weeks.
5. Record changes you see in the jar.

Think About It

1. What changes did you observe in the jar?
2. How does making compost help the environment?

Take It Home!

You can make a real compost bin at home. Ask an adult to help you find a spot to set up your bin. Measure the area before building your bin.

Start your compost pile with a layer of "brown stuff," such as leaves or pine needles. Then, add some "green stuff" — food scraps, grass clippings, and weeds. Mix the green stuff and brown stuff together. Top the whole thing off with a shovelful of soil. Remember to water each layer as you build the compost pile. Repeat each of the layers until the bin is full.

Soon you will be able to use your compost as mulch around garden plants or flowers. The mulch will give the plants the nutrients they need to grow!

PHYSICAL SCIENCE

The Inclined Plane

People often must move heavy things. Movers move boxes. Builders move lumber and tools. Drivers move things with their trucks. All that moving is a lot of work!

There are many kinds of machines that help move things. Some are very simple. A simple machine is a tool with a few or no moving parts. One simple machine is called an inclined plane.

An inclined plane has a flat surface. It is higher on one end. An inclined plane is used to move things.

Inclined planes make it easier to move things up or down. Ramps are inclined planes. Did you know that a slide is also an inclined plane? So is a road or a path that goes up a hill.

You can use an inclined plane to move all kinds of things. The boy in the picture is pushing the heavy box to make it slide up the ramp. It takes less force to slide the box up the ramp than to lift it up.

You can also use an inclined plane to move yourself! Which takes more energy — walking up a ladder or going down a slide? If you said walking up the ladder takes more energy, you are right.

Inclined planes make it easier to move just about anything. They let you move an object with less force.

Try It!

You can make your own inclined plane to help you move a heavy book. Follow the directions and see how it works!

What to Do

Part 1

1. Tie one end of the string around the book.
2. Hold the other end of the string in both hands.
3. Lift the book straight up until it is 30 cm above the floor. Have your partner measure 30 cm using the ruler.

Part 2

1. Make a stack of blocks 30 cm high.
2. Place one end of the board on the stack to create a ramp.
3. Place the book at the bottom of the ramp.
4. Hold the end of the string in both hands.
5. Pull the book up the ramp to the top. Have your partner steady the ramp to keep it from tipping.

Think About It

1. Which took more force, lifting the book or pulling it up the ramp?
2. How was the inclined plane helpful?

Take It Home!

People use inclined planes in their everyday lives. Look around your home for any inclined planes that you use. Think about others you may have seen. Describe some of them in a chart.

Inclined Plane	How I Use It
hill	pull up my wagon

Glossary/Glosario

The glossary uses letters and signs to show how words are pronounced. The mark ′ is placed after a syllable with a primary or heavy accent. The mark ′ is placed after a syllable with a secondary or lighter accent.

To hear the English words pronounced, listen to the AudioText CD.

adapt (ə dapt′) To change. Animals are **adapted** to live in their environment. (page 16)

adaptar Cambiar. Los animales están **adaptados** para vivir en su ambiente. (página 16)

amphibian (am fib′ē ən) An animal with bones that lives part of its life on land and part of its life in water. My pet frog is an **amphibian.** (page 41)

anfibio Animal con columna vertebral que vive parte de su vida en la tierra y parte de su vida en el agua. La rana que tengo de mascota es un **anfibio.** (página 41)

attract (ə trakt′) To pull toward. The opposite poles of two magnets will **attract** one another. (page 318)

atraer Jalar hacia sí. Los polos opuestos de un imán **se atraen** uno al otro. (página 318)

axis (ak′sis) An imaginary line around which a planet turns. Earth spins on an **axis.** (page 370)

eje Línea imaginaria sobre la cual gira un planeta. La Tierra gira sobre un **eje.** (página 370)

B

bird (bėrd) An animal with a backbone that has feathers, two legs, and wings. The **bird** flew from place to place searching for food. (page 40)

ave Animal con columna vertebral, que tiene plumas, dos patas y alas. El **ave** voló en busca de alimento. (página 40)

boulder (bōl′dər) A very big rock. The **boulder** is by the water. (page 146)

peña Una roca muy grande. Hay una **peña** junto al agua. (página 146)

camouflage (kam′ə fläzh) A color or shape that makes a plant or an animal hard to see. Some animals use **camouflage** to hide themselves from danger. (page 42)

camuflaje Color o forma que hace que un animal o planta sea difícil de ver. Algunos animales se **camuflan** para ocultarse de los peligros que los rodean. (página 42)

condense (kən dens′) To change from a gas to a liquid. Water vapor **condenses** on the outside of my glass of juice. (page 179)

condensarse Cambiar de gas a líquido. El vapor de agua **se condensó** por fuera de mi vaso de jugo. (página 179)

conductor (kən duk′tər)
Something that lets heat easily
move through it. Metal is a
conductor. (page 281)

conductor Algo que permite que
la energía se mueva fácilmente.
El metal es un **conductor.**
(página 281)

constellation (kon′stə lā′shən) A
group of stars that form a picture.
I like to search the night sky for
constellations. (page 376)

constelación Grupo de estrellas
que forman una figura. Me gusta
buscar **constelaciones** en el
cielo de noche. (página 376)

consumer (kən sü′mər) A living thing that cannot make its own food. Animals are **consumers.** (page 71)

consumidor Un consumidor es un ser vivo que no produce su propio alimento. Todos los animales son **consumidores.** (página 71)

crater (krā′tər) A hole that is shaped like a bowl. There are many **craters** on the surface of the Moon. (page 378)

cráter Agujero que tiene forma de tazón. En la superficie de la Luna hay muchos **cráteres.** (página 378)

dinosaur (dī′nə sôr) An extinct animal that lived millions of years ago. **Dinosaurs** are large animals that lived on Earth long ago. (page 212)

dinosaurio Reptil extinto que existió hace millones de años. Los **dinosaurios** fueron animales grandes que vivieron en la Tierra hace mucho tiempo. (página 212)

energy (en′ər jē) The ability to do work or make change. You need **energy** to play soccer. (page 271)

energía Capacidad de hacer trabajo o causar cambio. Necesitas **energía** para jugar fútbol. (página 271)

engine (en'jən) A machine that changes energy into force or motion. Cars, trains, and airplanes have an **engine** that helps them run. (page 400)

motor Máquina que transforma la energía en fuerza o movimiento. Los carros, los trenes y los aviones tienen un **motor** que los hace funcionar. (página 400)

environment (en vī'rən mənt) Everything that surrounds a living thing. A cactus is a plant that grows in a desert **environment.** (page 16)

ambiente Todo lo que rodea a un ser vivo. El cactus es una planta que crece en un **ambiente** de desierto. (página 16)

erosion (i rō′zhən) Process by which rocks and soil are moved from one place to another. Heavy rains can cause **erosion.** (page 152)

erosión Proceso por el cual se mueven rocas y pedazos de suelo de un lugar a otro. Las fuertes lluvias pueden producir **erosión.** (página 152)

evaporate (i vap′ə rāt′) To change from a liquid to a gas. The puddle of water will **evaporate** and turn into water vapor. (page 179)

evaporarse Cambiar de líquido a gas. Los charcos se **evaporan** cuando sale el Sol y se convierten en vapor de agua. (página 179)

extinct (ek stingkt′) An animal or plant no longer living on Earth. Dinosaurs are **extinct.** (page 210)

extinto Animal o planta que ya no existe en la Tierra. Los dinosaurios están **extintos.** (página 210)

F

fish (fish) An animal with bones that lives in water and has gills. Many types of **fish** live in an ocean. (page 40)

pez Animal con columna vertebral que vive en el agua y tiene branquias. En el mar viven muchos tipos de **peces.** (página 40)

flower (flou′ər) The part of a plant that makes seeds. Some plants have many **flowers.** (page 9)

flor La parte de la planta que produce las semillas. Algunas plantas tienen muchas **flores.** (página 9)

food chain (füd chān) Plants use sunlight, air, and water to make food. Animals eat the plants. Other animals eat those animals. This is called a food chain. A coyote and a mountain lion are part of a **food chain.** (page 74)

cadena alimentaria Las plantas utilizan la luz del Sol, aire y agua para producir su alimento. Los animales se comen las plantas. Luego, otros animales se comen a esos animales. Ésta es una cadena alimentaria. El coyote y el puma forman parte de una **cadena alimentaria.** (página 74)

food web (füd web) A food web is made up of the food chains in a habitat. Corn, voles, and foxes are part of a **food web.** (page 76)

red alimentaria Una red alimentaria se compone de las cadenas alimentarias de un hábitat. El maíz, la rata de campo y el zorro forman parte de una **red alimentaria.** (página 76)

force (fôrs) A push or pull that makes something move. You use **force** to move the wagon. (page 304)

fuerza El empujón o el jalón que hace que algo se mueva. Se aplica **fuerza** para mover el carrito. (página 304)

fossil (fos′əl) A print or remains of a plant or animal that lived long ago. Dinosaur **fossils** are in the museum. (page 207)

fósil Parte o huella de una planta o un animal que vivió hace mucho tiempo. En el museo hay **fósiles** de dinosaurio. (página 207)

friction (frik′shən) A force that slows down or stops moving objects. A bicycle's brakes use **friction** to slow down. (page 312)

fricción Fuerza que hace que un objeto en movimiento vaya más despacio o se detenga. Los frenos de una bicicleta usan **fricción** para bajar la velocidad. (página 312)

fuel (fyü′əl) Anything that is burned to make heat or power. We use wood as **fuel.** (page 279)

combustible Cualquier cosa que se quema para que dé calor o energía. Usamos madera como **combustible.** (página 279)

gas (gas) Matter that always takes the size and shape of its container. Bubbles are filled with **gas.** (page 246)

gas Materia que siempre llena el espacio del recipiente que la contiene. Las burbujas están llenas de **gas.** (página 246)

germinate (jėr′mə nāt) To begin to grow into a young plant. The plant seeds will soon **germinate.** (page 114)

germinar Comenzar a crecer para convertirse en una nueva planta. Las semillas pronto comenzarán a **germinar.** (página 114)

gills (gilz) Special body parts that get oxygen from water. Fish have **gills.** (page 46)

branquias Partes especiales del cuerpo de ciertos animales que los ayudan a obtener oxígeno del agua. Los peces tienen **branquias.** (página 46)

gravity (grav′ə tē) A force that pulls things toward the center of Earth. **Gravity** will pull the leaves back to Earth. (page 306)

gravedad Fuerza que jala los objetos hacia el centro de la Tierra. La **gravedad** hará que las hojas regresen a la Tierra. (página 306)

H

hibernate (hī′bər nāt) To spend all winter sleeping or resting. Some animals **hibernate.** (page 186)

hibernar Pasar todo el invierno durmiendo o descansando. Algunos animales **hibernan.** (página 186)

hurricane (hėr′ə kān) A storm that starts over warm ocean waters that has hard rain and very strong winds. A **hurricane** causes heavy rain and strong winds. (page 192)

huracán Tempestad que comienza en las aguas cálidas del mar, y que trae mucha lluvia y fuertes vientos. Un **huracán** causa fuertes lluvias y vientos. (página 192)

I

insect (in′sekt) An animal without bones that has three body parts and six legs. It's fun to watch **insects.** (page 52)

insecto Animal sin huesos, con el cuerpo dividido en tres partes y que tiene seis patas. Es muy divertido observar **insectos.** (página 52)

invent (in vent´) To make something for the first time. Alexander Graham Bell **invented** the telephone. (page 399)

inventar Hacer algo por primera vez. Alexander Graham Bell **inventó** el teléfono. (página 399)

L

leaves (lēvz) Parts of a plant that use sunlight, air, nutrients, and water to make food for the plant. The **leaves** on the plant are long and thin. (page 8)

hojas Las partes de una planta que usan luz del Sol, aire, nutrientes y agua para producir el alimento para la planta. Las **hojas** de la planta son largas y angostas. (página 8)

life cycle (līf sī′kəl) The way a living thing grows and changes. We studied the **life cycle** of a turtle. (page 106)

ciclo de vida El modo en que los seres vivos crecen y cambian. Hoy estudiamos **el ciclo de vida** de la tortuga. (página 106)

lightning (līt′ning) A flash of electricity in the sky. We watched **lightning** flash across the sky. (page 188)

rayo Una descarga luminosa de electricidad en el cielo. Vimos que un **rayo** cruzó el cielo. (página 188)

liquid (lik′wid) Matter that does not have its own shape, but does have its own mass. **Liquids** take the shape of their containers. (page 244)

líquido Materia que no tiene forma propia, pero tiene su propia masa. Los **líquidos** toman la forma del recipiente. (página 244)

loudness (loud′nəs) How loud or soft a sound is. The **loudness** of some sounds can change. (page 336)

intensidad Qué tan fuerte o suave es un sonido. La **intensidad** de algunos sonidos puede cambiar. (página 336)

mammal (mam′əl) An animal with bones that usually has hair or fur on its body and feeds milk to its young. Chipmunks are **mammals.** (page 40)

mamífero Animal con columna vertebral y cuerpo generalmente cubierto de pelo o pelaje, que alimenta a sus crías con su leche. Las ardillas rayadas son **mamíferos.** (página 40)

manufacture (man′yə fak′chər) To make by hand or machine. Many countries in the world **manufacture** clothing. (page 408)

manufacturar Producir cosas a mano o con máquinas. La ropa se **manufactura** en muchos países del mundo. (página 408)

mass (mas) The amount of matter in an object. I use a balance to measure **mass.** (page 239)

masa La cantidad de materia que tiene un objeto. Uso una balanza para medir la **masa.** (página 239)

meteorologist (mē′tē ə rol′ə jist) A person who studies weather. The **meteorologist** predicted sunny weather. (page 407)

meteorólogo Persona que estudia el estado del tiempo. La **meteoróloga** anunció tiempo soleado. (página 407)

migrate (mī′grāt) To move from one place to another in a regular pattern. Many types of birds **migrate** in the winter. (page 184)

migrar Mudarse de un lugar a otro siguiendo un patrón determinado. Muchos tipos de aves **migran** en el invierno. (página 184)

mineral (min′ər əl) A nonliving solid that comes from Earth. Copper is a **mineral.** (page 147)

mineral Sólido sin vida que proviene de la Tierra. El cobre es un **mineral.** (página 147)

mixture (miks′chər) Something made up of two or more kinds of matter that do not change. Fruit salad is a **mixture** of different fruits. (page 250)

mezcla Algo hecho de dos o más tipos de materia que no cambian. Esta ensalada es una **mezcla** de frutas. (página 250)

motion (mō′shen) Motion is the act of moving. A merry-go-round moves in a circular **motion.** (page 303)

movimiento Movimiento es el acto de cambiar de posición. Los carruseles siguen un **movimiento** circular. (página 303)

natural resource (nach′ər əl rē′sôrs) A useful thing that comes from nature. Rocks are **natural resources.** (page 143)

recurso natural Una cosa útil que proviene de la naturaleza. Las rocas son un **recurso natural.** (página 143)

nutrients (nü′trē ənts) Materials that living things need to live and grow. People get **nutrients** from the food they eat. (page 7)

nutrientes Sustancias que los seres vivos necesitan para vivir y crecer. Las personas obtenemos **nutrientes** del alimento que consumimos. (página 7)

nymph (nimf) A young insect that looks like its parent and grows wings as it changes. We found a dragonfly **nymph** in the pond by our school. (page 108)

ninfa Insecto joven que se parece a sus padres, pero que no tiene alas. Nos encontramos una **ninfa** de libélula en la charca que hay junto a nuestra escuela. (página 108)

orbit (ôr′bit) The path around something. It takes Earth about one year to **orbit** the Sun one time. (page 374)

órbita El camino alrededor de algo. La Tierra tarda aproximadamente un año en recorrer una **órbita** completa alrededor del Sol. (página 374)

paleontologist (pā′lē on tol′ə jist)
A scientist who studies fossils.
Paleontologists study fossils
to learn about life long ago.
(page 207)

paleontólogo Científico
que estudia los fósiles. Los
paleontólogos estudian fósiles
para saber cómo era la vida hace
mucho tiempo. (página 207)

phase (fāz) The shape of the
lighted part of the Moon. The
Moon's **phases** can be seen
best at night. (page 381)

fase La forma de la parte
iluminada de la Luna. Las **fases**
de la Luna se pueden ver mejor de
noche. (página 381)

pitch (pich) How high or low a sound is. The sound from the bullfrog had a low **pitch.** (page 338)

tono Qué tan agudo o tan grave es un sonido. El sonido que hace una rana es de **tono** grave. (página 338)

pollution (pə lü′shən) Anything harmful added to land, air, or water. Many people work hard to reduce **pollution.** (page 154)

contaminación Cualquier cosa dañina que se le pone a la tierra, al agua o al aire. Muchas personas se esfuerzan por reducir la **contaminación.** (página 154)

prairie (prâr′ē) Flat land covered with grasses and having few trees. A **prairie** has a lot of grass and few trees. (page 20)

pradera Tierra plana cubierta de hierbas y donde hay pocos árboles. En una **pradera** hay muchas hierbas y pocos árboles. (página 20)

predator (pred′ə tər) An animal that catches and eats another animal for food. A lion is a **predator.** (page 75)

predador Un animal que caza a otros animales para alimentarse. El león es un feroz **predador.** (página 75)

prey (prā) An animal that is caught and eaten for food. Sea stars are the **prey** of sea otters. (page 75)

presa Un animal al que se caza y sirve de alimento. La estrella de mar es la **presa** de las nutrias de mar. (página 75)

producer (prə dü′sər) A living thing that makes its own food. A kelp is a **producer.** (page 71)

productor Un ser vivo que produce su propio alimento. Una planta verde es un **productor.** (página 71)

property (prop′ər tē) Something about an object that you can observe with your senses. An object's color is one kind of **property.** (page 240)

propiedad Algo en un objeto que puedes observar con tus sentidos. El color de un objeto es una **propiedad** de ese objeto. (página 240)

R

recycle (rē sī′kəl) To change something so that it can be used again. My family **recycles** plastic bottles. (page 156)

reciclar Transformar algo para poder usarlo otra vez. En mi familia **reciclamos** las botellas plásticas. (página 156)

reflect (ri flekt′) To bounce off of something. A mirror can **reflect** light. (page 282)

reflejarse Rebotar en algo. La luz **se refleja** en el espejo. (página 282)

repel (ri pel′) To push away. The north ends of magnets will **repel** one another. (page 318)

repeler Empujar para apartar de sí. Los polos norte de dos imanes se **repelen** uno al otro. (página 318)

reptile (rep′tīl) An animal with bones that has dry, scaly skin. Snakes are **reptiles.** (page 41)

reptil Animal con columna vertebral, cubierto de piel seca y escamosa. Las serpientes son **reptiles.** (página 41)

roots (rüts) Parts of a plant that hold the plant in place and that take in water and nutrients from the soil. The **roots** of the old oak tree are deep inside the ground. (page 8)

raíces Partes que sostienen a una planta dentro de la tierra, y que absorben agua y nutrientes del suelo. Las **raíces** del viejo roble están bajo tierra a mucha profundidad. (página 8)

rotation (rō tā′shən) Spinning on an axis. Earth makes one complete **rotation** each day. (page 370)

rotación El acto de girar sobre un eje. La Tierra tarda un día en completar una **rotación** sobre su eje. (página 370)

S

sand (sand) Tiny pieces of rock. People use **sand** to build roads. (page 146)

arena Pedacitos muy pequeños de roca. Las personas usan **arena** para construir calles. (página 146)

satellite (sat′l ĭt) An object that revolves around another object. Meteorologists study pictures taken by **satellites** to predict weather. (page 407)

satélite Objeto que gira alrededor de otro objeto. Los meteorólogos predicen el estado del tiempo con fotos tomadas desde **satélites.** (página 407)

seed coat (sēd kōt) The hard outer covering of a seed. The **seed coat** protects the seed. (page 114)

envoltura de la semilla Cubierta dura que tienen las semillas por fuera. La **envoltura de la semilla** protege la semilla. (página 114)

seedling (sēd′ling) A young plant. The tree **seedling** grows into a tree. (page 114)

plántula Una planta joven. La **plántula** crece y se convierte en un árbol. (página 114)

shadow (shad′ō) A shadow is made when something blocks the light. The tree makes a **shadow.** (page 284)

sombra Algo que se forma cuando algo bloquea la luz. El árbol hace una **sombra** en el suelo. (página 284)

simple machine (sim′pəl mə shēn) A tool with few or no moving parts that makes work easier. Workers often use **simple machines** to help them build things. (page 314)

máquina simple Herramienta que tiene pocas o ninguna parte móvil y que facilita el trabajo. Los trabajadores muchas veces usan **máquinas simples** para facilitarse el trabajo cuando construyen cosas. (página 314)

solar energy (sō′lər en′ərjē)
Solar energy is heat and light
from the Sun. The house is heated
by **solar energy.** (page 272)

energía solar El calor y la luz
provenientes del Sol. En mi
casa usamos **energía solar.**
(página 272)

solar system (sō′lər sis′tem)
The Sun, the planets and their
moons, and other objects that
orbit the Sun. Earth is in our
solar system. (page 382)

sistema solar El Sol, los planetas
y sus lunas, y otros astros que
giran alrededor del Sol. La Tierra
está en nuestro **sistema solar.**
(página 382)

solid (sol′id) Matter that has its own shape and takes up space. The case that holds the supplies is a **solid.** (page 242)

sólido Materia que tiene forma propia y ocupa espacio. La caja de útiles de pintura es un **sólido.** (página 242)

source (sôrs) A place from which something comes. A lamp is one **source** of light. (page 278)

fuente Lugar de donde proviene algo. Una lámpara es una **fuente** de luz. (página 278)

states of matter (stāts uv mat′ər)
The three states of matter are
solids, liquids, and gases. Water
is a liquid **state of matter.**
(page 242)

estados de la materia Los tres
estados en que se encuentra la
materia son sólido, líquido y
gaseoso. El agua se presenta en
el **estado de la materia** de
líquido. (página 242)

stem (stem) Part of a plant that
holds it up and that carries water
and nutrients to the leaves. The
stem is long and green. (page 8)

tallo La parte que sostiene a una
planta hacia arriba, y lleva agua
y nutrientes a las hojas. El **tallo**
es largo y verde. (página 8)

technology (tek nol′ə jē) Using science to help solve problems. People use **technology** every day. (page 399)

tecnología El uso de la ciencia para resolver problemas. Usamos la **tecnología** todos los días. (página 399)

tornado (tôr nā′dō) Very strong wind that comes down from clouds in the shape of a funnel. A **tornado** touched down near our town. (page 190)

tornado Viento muy fuerte que baja de las nubes en forma de embudo. Un **tornado** pasó cerca de nuestra ciudad. (página 190)

transportation (tran′spər tā′ shən) Ways to move people or things from place to place. Today, **transportation** makes travel easier and faster than ever before. (page 400)

transporte Medios para mover personas o cosas. Hoy en día, el **transporte** nos permite viajar con más rapidez y facilidad que nunca. (página 400)

vaccine (vak sēn′) Medicine that can help prevent a disease. Mia got a shot of the flu **vaccine.** (page 402)

vacuna Medicina que puede prevenir una enfermedad. A María le pusieron una **vacuna** contra la gripe. (página 402)

vibrate (vī′brāt) To move back and forth very fast. A flute makes the air **vibrate** to make sounds. (page 335)

vibrar Moverse muy rápido hacia adelante y hacia atrás. La flauta hace **vibrar** el aire para producir sonidos. (página 335)

water cycle (wȯ′tər sī′kəl) The way water moves from the clouds to Earth and back to the clouds. Water condenses and evaporates during the **water cycle.** (page 178)

ciclo del agua El movimiento del agua de la Tierra al aire y nuevamente hacia la Tierra. El agua se condensa y se evapora durante el **ciclo del agua.** (página 178)

weathering (we′ᵺər ing) The breaking apart and changing of rocks. **Weathering** causes sharp rocks to become smooth. (page 153)

meteorización Cuando las rocas se rompen y cambian. La **meteorización** hace que las rocas afiladas queden lisas. (página 153)

work (wėrk) When force moves an object. It took a lot of **work** to push the sled up the hill. (page 308)

trabajo Cuando una fuerza hace mover un objeto. Costó mucho **trabajo** arrastrar el trineo loma arriba. (página 308)

This Index lists the pages on which topics appear in this book. Page numbers after a *p* refer to a photograph. Page numbers after a *c* refer to a chart or graph.

Activities

directed inquiry, explore. *See* Directed Inquiry, Explore

guided inquiry, investigate. *See* Guided Inquiry, Investigate

take-home. *See* Take-home Activities

Adapt, adaptation, 16–25

Air, as natural resource, 142–145

Alike and different, 37, 41, 45, 117, 120–121, 131, 140, 218–219, 365, 369, 389

Amphibians, *p*35, *p*41, *p*50–51

Animal scientist, 352

Animals

functions, of body parts, 316–317

grouping, 58–59, 131

growth and change, 102–113

interdependence, 84–89

needs of, 71–73, 274–277

and plants, 84–86

protecting, 158–159

sounds of, 342–343

Antarctica, 62–63

Ants, *p*84

Art in science, 14, 43, 75, 117, 157, 182, 188, 251, 283, 319, 341, 379

Astronaut, 262–263

Astronomer, 392

Atmospheric scientist, 200

Attract, attraction, *p*299, 318, *p*319, *p*320, *p*321

Axis, *p*362, *p*370, *p*371

Backbones

animals with, 39–51

animals without, 52–55

Bar graph, 348–349

Biographies

Hendrickson, Susan, 224

Jenkins, Luther, 328

Mota, Mario J., 128

Purgue, Alejandro, 352

Wright, Shonte, 416

Birds, *p*40, *p*44, *p*45

Bones, 38–39. *See also* Backbones

Boulders, *p*138, *p*146

Build background, 2–3, 34–35, 66–67, 98–99, 138–139, 170–171, 202–203, 234–235, 266–267, 298–299, 330–331, 362–363, 394–395

Cactus, *p*13, *p*23, *p*116

Camouflage, *p*35, *p*42, *p*44, *p*52

Careers

astronomer, 392

atmospheric scientist, 200

farmer, 96

forester, 168

lighting operator, 296

marine biologist, 128

material scientist, 264

plant scientist, 32

wildlife rehabilitator, 64

Cause and effect, 69, 73, 83, 95

Chameleon, p48

Chapter reviews. *See* Reviews, chapter

Chase, Mary Agnes, 32

Chipmunk, p43

Clay soil, p148, 149

Communicating, 56–57, 131, 204, 205, 223, 300, 301, 327, 389, 396, 397

Communication, and technology, 404–405

Condense, condensation, p179

Conductor, p280–281

Conservation, 154–159

Constellations, p376, p377, 384–385

Consumers, p71

Crater, p378–379

Data

collecting, 100, 122–123, 194–195, 199, 228–229

interpreting, 194–195, 322–323

recording, 122–123, 228–229

Day and night, 370–371

Deer, p42, p58

Desert, 22, p23

Dinosaurs, p202–203, 212–217, 223

Directed inquiry, explore, 4, 68, 100, 140, 172, 204, 236, 268, 300, 332, 365, 396

Diving beetle, p52–53

Dragonfly, p108, p109

Drawing conclusions, 173, 179, 184, 192, 199, 237, 247, 249, 261

Drought, p177

Earth, 152, p382, 386

Effect, and cause. *See* Cause and effect

Electricity, 288–289

Energy, p266, 271, 274–277

Engine, p400

Engineer, 328

Environment, of plants, 16

Erosion, p152, 153

Estimating and measuring, 17, 89, 92–93, 124–125, 147, 217, 220–221, 232, 243, 256–257, 258–259, 292–293, 300, 311, 324–325

Evaporate, evaporation, p179, 251, 254–255

Experiment. *See* Full Inquiry, Experiment

Experimenting. *See* Directed Inquiry, Explore; Full Inquiry, Experiment; Guided Inquiry, Investigate

Explore. *See* Directed Inquiry, Explore

Extinct, 210

Fair test, plan a, 132–133, 136, 228–229, 232, 356–357, 360, 420–421, 424

Fall season, p184, 185

Ferns, 14, p15

Fish, p40, p46–47

Flowers, p2, p9, 12, 13, p117

Flying squirrels, p42–43

Food

as energy, 276–277

in space, 262–263

Food chain, p67, 74–75, 78–79

Food web, 67, 76–83

changing, 82–83

ocean, 80–81

Force, 304–305

Forester, 168

Fossil, p202, 207–211, 218–219, 220–221, 223

Freezing, 252–253

Friction, p312–313

Frog, p41, p50, p51

Fruit, p12

Fuel, p279

Full inquiry, experiment, 132–133, 228–229, 356–357, 420–421

Gaffer, 296

Gas, 246–247, 253, 254–255

Geography, 85, 181, 183, 185, 187

Germinate, 99, p114

Gills, p34, p46

Giraffe, p71

Graphing, 58–59, 100, 220–221, 348–349

Grassland, 74–77

Gravity, p306, p307

Growth and change

animals, 102–113

human beings, 118–121

insects, 108–109, 122–123

plants, 114–117

Guided inquiry, investigate, 26–27, 56–57, 90–91, 122–123, 160–161, 194–195, 218–219, 256–257, 290–291, 322–323, 346–347, 384–385, 410–411

H

Habitats, 72–73

Health in science, 13, 155, 276, 402–403

Heat, 278–281

Heating matter, 254, p255

Hendrickson, Susan, 224

Hibernate, hibernation, 43, p171, p186

Horse, p110–111

How to Read Science

alike and different, 37, 365

cause and effect, 69

drawing conclusions, 173, 237

important details, 333

infer, 101, 269

picture clues, 141

predict, 5

put things in order, 301

retell, 205, 397

Hubble **space telescope,** 392

Human beings

growth and change, 118–121

needs of, 274–277

Hummingbirds, p44

Humus, p148, p149

Hurricanes, p171, p192–193

Hypothesis, make a, 132–133, 228–229, 356–357, 420–421

Iguana, *p*49

Important details, 333, 338, 343, 351

Inclined plane, *p*315

Inferring, 26–27, 31, 68, 90–91, 100, 109, 122–123, 127, 172, 173, 236, 237, 268, 269, 274, 289, 290–291, 295, 415

Insect, *p*35, *p*52–53, 55
life cycles, *p*108–109, 122–123

Internet, using, 159, 177, 387

Invent, 399

Investigate. *See* Guided Inquiry, Investigate

Jenkins, Luther, 328

Krill, *p*63

Leaves, *p*3, *p*8, 14, *p*28–29

Lever, *p*314, *p*316

Life cycle,
bean plant, *p*114–115
butterfly, *p*122, *p*124
dragonfly, *p*108–109
frog, *p*125
horse, *p*110–111
sea turtle, 104–107, *p*106–107

Light, 282–283

Lighting operator, 296

Lightning, *p*188–189

Liquids, *p*244–245, *p*252, *p*253, *p*255, 340–341

Loudness, *p*336, *p*337

Magnet, 318–321, 322–323

Mammal, *p*34, 38–39, *p*40, *p*42–43

Manufacture, 395, *p*408, *p*409

Map, *c*181, *c*183, *c*185, *c*187

Marine biologist, 128

Mars, *p*382, 383, 386–387, *p*390–391

Marsh, 24–25

Mass, 239, *p*242

Material scientist, 264

Math in science, 17, 47, 55, 77, 89, 105, 115, 147, 217, 241, 243, 253, 285, 311, 381, 405
bar graph, 162–163, 348–349
comparing numbers, 412–413
estimating and measuring, 92–93, 124–125, 220–221, 258–259, 292–293, 324–325, 348–349
graphing and charting, 162–163, 196–197, 220–221, 258–259, 292–293, 348–349, 386–387, 412–413
grouping and sorting, 58–59
number sentences, 162–163, 324–325
patterns, 28–29

Matter, 239–261
changing, 248–255
properties of, *p*240–241
states of, 242–249, 353

Maze, making a, 410–411

Measuring and estimating,
See Estimating and measuring

Melting, 254, *p*255

Mercury, p382, p386, 387

Meteorologist, p407

Migrate, migration, 184, p185

Mineral, p147

Mixture, p250, p251

Models, making and using, 36, 90–91, 123, 218–219, 365, 384–385

Moon, the, 378–381

Mosses, 14, p15

Mota, Mario J., 128

Motion, 303, p303, p313

   and force, 310–311

   measuring, 324–325

NASA (National Aeronautics and Space Administration)

   careers at, 128, 200, 264, 328, 416

   mission to Mars, 390–391

   satellites, 62, p63, 166–167, p166, p167

   space food, 262–263

   studies penguins, 62–63

Natural resources, 143–151

Neptune, 382, p383, 386, p387

Nests, building, p86, p87

Night and day, p370, p371

NOAA (National Oceanic and Atmospheric Administration) Web site, 177

Nutrients, 7, 8, 24

Nymph, p108, 109

Observing, xxii, xxvii, 26–27, 132–133, 140, 141, 160–161, 165, 218–219, 228–229, 256–257, 261, 290–291, 295, 322–323, 332, 333, 351, 356–357, 384–385, 410–411

Octopus, p54, 56–57, p58

Oil spill, p82, p83

Operational definitions, making, 384–385

Opportunity (space rover), p391

Orbit, p374–375, c386, 387

Paleontologist, p207, 224

Patterns, p28, p29

Penguins, p45, p62–63

Peticolas, Laura, 392

Phase, p380–381

Picture clues, 141, 148–149, 150–151, 165

Pinecones, 14, p15

Pitch, p338–339

Plants

   and animals, 84–87

   classifying, 12–15

   environment, 16–17

   life cycles, p114–115, 116, 117

   as natural resource, p150–151

   needs of, 4, 7, 26–27, 71–73, 144–145, 274–275

   parts of, p8–9

   protecting, 158–159

   woodland, 16–19

Poems

   "Apple Shadows," 358–359

   "Little Seeds," 134–135

   "The Spring Wind," 230–231

   "This Happy Day," 422–423

Pollution, p154–155, 401

Prairie, p20–21

Predator, p75

Predict, 4, 5, 10, 31, 256–257, 322–323, 346–347, 410–411

Prey, p75

Producer, 71

Properties, of matter, p240–241

Pulley, p315

Purgue, Alejandro, 352

Put things in order, 301, 307, 312, 327

Rainfall, 172

Recycling, p156–157, 162–163

Reflect, reflection, p282, p283

Repel, 318, p319

Reptiles, p41, p48, p49

Retell, 205, 209, 211, 223, 397, 403, 409, 415

Reviews, chapter, 30–31, 60–61, 94–95, 126–127, 164–165, 198–199, 222–223, 260–261, 294–295, 326–327, 350–351, 388–389, 414–415

Reviews, unit

Performance Assessment, 131, 227, 355, 419

Test Talk, 129, 225, 353, 417

Wrap-Up, 130, 226, 354, 418

Rock, p146, 147

Root, p8, 14

Rotation, of planets, 370, p371

Sand, p138, 146

Satellites, space, 62, p63, 166, p167, p407

Saturn, 382, p383, 386–387

Science Fair Projects, 136, 232, 360, 424

Science process skills

classify, 194–195

collect data, 100, 122–123, 199, 229

communicate, 56–57, 61, 204, 205, 223, 300, 301, 327, 389, 396, 397, 411

control variables, 132–133

estimate and measure, 68, 256, 300, 421

infer, 27, 31, 68, 69, 90–91, 95, 100, 101, 123, 127, 133, 161, 172, 173, 219, 236, 237, 268, 269, 346–347, 415

interpret data, 322–323

investigate. See Guided inquiry, investigate

make and use models, 36, 37, 90, 91, 132, 218–219, 364, 365, 384

make definitions, 384–385

make hypotheses, 132, 228–229, 356, 420

observe, 26, 27, 133, 140, 141, 160, 165, 218–219, 229, 236, 256, 261, 290–291, 295, 323, 332, 333, 356, 385, 410

plan a fair test, 132, 228, 356, 420

predict, 4, 5, 56, 123, 322, 346–347, 410–411

Scientific methods, using, xxvi, 136, 232, 360, 424

Sea otter, p79

Seasons, 180–187, 196–197, 199, 374–375

Seed coat, p114, 115

Seedling, 114, p115

Seed, p9, 10, p11, 14, 114

Shadow, p284–285, 292–293

Shelter, p86, p87

Simple machines, p314–315

Skunks, p38, p39

Sky, 376–379

Snake, 36, p37, p48

Social studies in science, 18, 22, 85, 107, 279, 286, 315, 374

Soil, 140, 141, p148, p149, 228–229

Solar energy, p272, p273

Solar system, 382–387, p382–383

Solids, 242–243, 252–253, 340–341

Songs

"Go Find a Fossil," 206

"Good Partners," 70

"Hi Little Turtle," 102

"Listen to the Sounds," 334

"Natural Resources," 142

"Plants," 6

"Technology Helps Us All," 398

"The Sun," 366

"They're All Matter!," 238

"Use Some Force!," 302

"What Has Backbones?," 38

"What's the Weather?," 174

"Where Do We Get Energy?," 270

Sound, 336–345

Source, of heat, p278

Space food, 262–263

Space rovers, 390, p391, p416

Spiders, p55

Spring season, 180, p181

Stars, p376, p377

Stems, p9, 14

Summer, 182, p183

Sun, the, 367–375

197, 200, 221, 224, 259, 263, 264, 293, 296, 325, 328, 349, 352, 387, 391, 392, 413, 416

Target Reading Skills

alike and different, 37, 41, 45, 61, 365, 369, 383, 389

cause and effect, 69, 73, 83, 95

draw conclusions, 173, 179, 184, 192, 199, 237, 247, 249, 261

important details, 333, 338, 343, 351

infer, 101, 109, 111, 121, 127, 269, 274, 289, 295

picture clues, 141, 149, 151, 165

predict, 5, 10, 24, 31

put things in order, 301, 307, 312, 327

retell, 205, 209, 211, 223, 397, 403, 409, 415

Technology, 399

Technology in science, 53, 159, 177, 317, 376

Temperature, measuring, 256–257

Thunderstorm, p188–189

Time, measuring, 124–125

Toads, p51

Tornadoes, p190–191

Transportation, p400–401

Trees, p12, p16, p17

Turtles, p64, 102–107

life cycle, 104–107

Take-home activities, 29, 32, 59, 63, 64, 93, 96, 125, 128, 163, 167, 168,

Unit reviews. See Reviews, unit

Uranus, 382, p383, 386–387

Vaccine, p402

Venus, p382, p383, 386–387

Vibrate, vibration, 335

Vocabulary, 3, 35, 67, 99, 139, 171, 203, 235, 267, 299, 331, 363, 395

Water, as natural resource, 144–145

Water cycle, p178–179

Water vapor, 179, 252–253

Weather, 175–197

Weathering, 153

Wedge, p314, p316

Wheel and axle, p314–315

Wildlife rehabilitator, 64

Winter, 186, p187

Woodland habitat, p16, p17, p18–19

Work, p308–309

Wright, Shonte, 416

Writing in science, 9, 20, 31, 49, 51, 61, 79, 81, 87, 95, 111, 113, 127, 144, 153, 165, 180, 186, 190, 199, 213, 215, 223, 245, 255, 261, 273, 281, 295, 305, 309, 321, 327, 337, 344, 351, 371, 373, 389, 401, 407, 415

Yeast, p68, 69

Credits

Illustrations

29, 301, 327, 362, 367–368, 370–374, 376, 378, 380, 382, 388 Bob Kayganich; 69 Patrick Gnan; 201–203, 205–208 Big Sesh Studios; 344 Philip Williams; 365 Mary Teichman.

Photographs

Every effort has been made to secure permission and provide appropriate credit for photographic material. The publisher deeply regrets any omission and pledges to correct errors called to its attention in subsequent editions.

Unless otherwise acknowledged, all photographs are the property of Pearson Education, Inc.

Photo locators denoted as follows: Top (T), Center (C), Bottom (B), Left (L), Right (R), Background (Bkgd)

Cover: (C) ©Chase Swift/Corbis, (Bkgrd) ©Ralph A. Clevenger/Corbis, (B) ©Walter Hodges/Corbis;

Text

iii (T, B) DK Images; **v** DK Images; **vi** (R, L) Fotolia; **vii** (B) Fotolia, (T) Thinkstock; **viii** (T, B) Fotolia; **ix** (T) Thinkstock; **x** (B) DK Images, (R, L) Fotolia; **xi** (T) Fotolia; **xiii** DK Images; **xiv** (T) Thinkstock; **xv** ©Pavel Losevsky/Fotolia; **xvi** (R, L) Fotolia; **xvii** Fotolia; **xviii** (T, B) /NASA; **xix** ©minicel73/Fotolia; **xxi** (R) Fotolia, (L) Sebastian Duda/Fotolia; **xxii** (C) JPL/Cornell University/NASA; **xxiii** (Inset) innovari/Fotolia; **xxiv** (Bkgrd) NASA; **xxv** (Inset) Digital Vision/Thinkstock; **xxix** (BR) © Royalty-Free/Corbis; **xxxi** (BR) Yuri Arcurs/Fotolia; **EM002** (B) Fotoimpressionen/Fotolia; **EM004** (Inset) Getty Images; **EM006** (b) image100/Getty Images; **EM011** (T) Sebastian Duda/Fotolia; **EM012** (B) © Royalty-Free/Corbis, (C) Fotolia; **EM013** Fotolia; **EM014** (B) Fotolia, (T) Thinkstock; **EM015** (T) Fotolia, (B) NASA; **EM016** (B) BananaStock/Thinkstock, (T) DK Images; **EM017** Fotolia; **EM018** Fotolia; **EM019** Jupiterimages/Thinkstock; **EM020** (BR, BL) ©Royalty-Free/Corbis, (T) DK Images, (B) Fotolia, (BC) Tom Brakefield/Thinkstock; **EM021** (TL) © Royalty-Free/Corbis, (TR) DK Images, (CR, C, B) Fotolia; **EM022** (T) DK Images, (B) Thinkstock; **EM023** (T) Thinkstock; **EM024** DK Images; **EM025** (T) Fotolia, (B) Jupiterimages/Thinkstock; **EM026** (B) DK Images, (T) Thinkstock; **EM027** DK Images; **EM028** (TR, TL) Fotolia, (B) SuperStock; **EM029** (B) Ralf Kraft/Fotolia; **EM030** ©Jiri Foltyn/Fotolia; **EM031** (B) Lisa F. Young/Fotolia; **EM032** (T) Fotolia, (B) Tyler Boyes/Fotolia; **EM033** (B) Fotolia; **EM034** Fotolia; **EM035** (T) Fotolia; **EM036** (B) Fotolia, (T) Paul Moore/Fotolia; **EM037** (B) Fotolia, (T) Thinkstock; **EM038** (B) Fotolia, (T) SuperStock; **EM039** (T) Fotolia, (T) Jupiter Images/Thinkstock; **EM040** Thinkstock; **EM041** (B) Chaucashoot/Fotolia, (T) Fotolia; **EM042** (T) DK Images; **EM043** (T) Fotolia, (B) Terry Morris/Fotolia; **EM044** DK Images, (B) Kim Taylor and Jane Burton/©DK Images; **EM045** (T) atomicrooster/Fotolia; **EM046** (B) Fotolia, (T) Getty Images; **EM048** DK Images; **EM049** Thinkstock; **EM050** (T) Fotolia, (B) Scott Van Blarcom/Fotolia; **EM051** (B) Thinkstock; **EM052** (T, B) Fotolia; **Unit A Opener** (Inset) Getty Images; **Unit B Opener** Mike Norton/Fotolia; **Unit C Opener** (Bkgrd) Sebastian Duda/Fotolia.

Unit D Opener (Inset) NASA;

1 (Inset, Bkgrd) Fotolia; **2** (B) DK Images; **3** (BL) DK Images, (BR) SuperStock; **5** (Inset) Fotolia, (C) Rlat/Fotolia; **6** (Inset) Fotolia; **7** (TL) Hemera Technologies, (BR) Jupiter Images; **8** (TL, C) DK Images; **10** (T) Comstock/Thinkstock, (TL) Jupiter Images, (C) Stephen Vonhorn/Fotolia, (B) Yuriy Vahlenko/Fotolia; **11** (BR) DK Images, (TR) Peter Chadwick/©DK Images, (CR) Steve Lovegrove/Fotolia; **12** (R) Jupiter Images/Thinkstock, (TL) Peter Anderson/DK Images; **13** (R) Bill Florence/Fotolia, (L) Thinkstock; **14** (T) Lake Erickson/Fotolia, (C) Liquid Library/Thinkstock; **15** (TR, CR) DK Images, (BR) Getty Images, (B) Jupiter Images /Thinkstock; **16** (TL) DK Images, (L) pitrs /Fotolia; **17** (L) Corbis, (R) DK Images; **18** (Bkgrd) Les Cunliffe/Fotolia, (Inset) Stockbyte/Thinkstock, (TL) Uhland/Fotolia; **19** (T, B) DK Images; **20** (R) SuperStock; **21** (B) Ed Baumgarten/Fotolia, (Bkgrd) Maro Markovi/Fotolia, (T) SuperStock; **22** (TL) Getty Images, (Bkgrd) Rusty Dodson/Fotolia, (R) Thinkstock; **23** (B) SuperStock, (T) Thinkstock; **24** (TL) Brand X Pictures/Getty Images, (Bkgrd) nick barounis/Fotolia; **25** (B) Asoby/Fotolia, (T) Peter Kirschner/Fotolia; **26** (Inset) selene7/Fotolia; **28** (T) Fotolia, (C, B) Matthew Ward/DK Images; **29** (Bkgrd) Fotolia; **30** (TL, CR, CL, BL) DK Images, (TR, BR) SuperStock; **31** (T) Peter Chadwick/©DK Images, (B) SuperStock; **32** (Inset) Jupiterimages/Thinkstock, (Bkgrd) Prints and Photographs Division/Prints & Photographs Division, Library of Congress; **33** (Bkgrd) Thinkstock; **34** (BL) Fotolia, (TR) Jupiterimages/Thinkstock, (T) Thinkstock; **35** (TR) Chaucashoot/Fotolia, (BL) Fotolia, (CR) Sebastian Duda/Fotolia, (BR) Valeriy Kirsanov/Fotolia; **37** (T) Jupiter Images, (B) Jupiter Images/ Getty Images/Thinkstock, (Bkgrd) Thinkstock, (C) Vinicius Tupinamba/Fotolia; **38** Thinkstock; **39** (B) Comstock/Thinkstock, (T) DK Images; **40** (BC) A.K. Wulff/Fotolia, (BL) Bruce MacQueen/Fotolia, (TL) Hemera Technologies, (BR) Thinkstock; **41** (L) Fotolia, (R) Sebastian Duda/Fotolia; **42** (T) ©Jupiterimages/Thinkstock, (BL) Corbis, (TL) Getty Images, (BR) Tom Brakefield/Thinkstock; **43** (R) Janet Thorpe/Fotolia; **44** (TL, BR) DK Images, (TR) Eduardo Rivero/Fotolia, (B) Fotolia; **46** (TL) ©Comstock, (BR, BL) DK Images; **47** (T, B) DK Images; **48** (T) Cathy Keifer/Fotolia, (B) Fotolia, (TL) Hemera Technologies; **49** (R) Gert Hochmuth/Fotolia; **50** (TL) Hemera Technologies, (B) Sebastian Duda/Fotolia; **51** (L) Getty Images, (R) Jupiterimages/gettyimages/Thinkstock; **52** (TR, TL) DK Images, (B) Fotolia; **54** (TL, R) DK Images; **55** (BR) Ablestock/Fotolia, (TR) DK Images; **56** (Inset) Ribe/Fotolia; **58** (BL) Corbis, (TR, TC, BC) DK Images, (TL) Sebastian Duda/Fotolia; **59** (L) DK Images, (R) Fotolia; **60** (BC) Jupiterimages/Thinkstock; (TL) Sebastian Duda/Fotolia; (TR) Fotolia, (CR) Bruce MacQueen/Fotolia, (CL) DK Images; (BL) Thinkstock; (BR) Fotolia; **61** (T) DK Images, (BR, BL) Hemera Technologies; **62** (B) Tom Brakefield/Thinkstock; **63** (TR) Jamie Hall/NOAA, (BR) Scientific Visualization Studio Collection/NASA; **64** (B) Kennedy Center Media Archive Collection/NASA, (T) Charles Dyer/Fotolia, (C) Richard Carey/Fotolia; **65** (Bkgrd) Fotolia; **66** (T) Fotolia, (B) Jupiter Images/Thinkstock; **67** (TR, TL, TC, CL, BR, BL) Fotolia, (CR) Goran Bogicevic/Fotolia; **69** (Bkgrd) Fotolia, (Inset) Getty Images; **70** Fotolia; **71** (TR) Hemera Technologies; **72** (B) Fotolia, (TL) Getty Images; **73** (TR) Anup Shah/Thinkstock; **74** (BL) ©Royalty-Free/Corbis, (BR) Fotolia, (TL) Frank Greenaway/DK Images; **75** (BR) Fotolia, (BL) Tom Brakefield/Thinkstock; **76** (CL) ©Royalty-Free/Corbis, (TR) DK Images, (TL) Eric Isselée/Fotolia, (C, B) Fotolia; **77** (BR) ©Royalty-Free/Corbis, (T) Sly/Fotolia, (BL) Tom Brakefield/Thinkstock; **78** (CL, B) Fotolia, (CR) Goran Bogicevic/Fotolia, (TL) Jupiter Images; **79** (B) the h/Fotolia; **80** (TC, CR, CL) Fotolia, (TL, B) Goran Bogicevic/Fotolia; **81** (TR, TL, B) Fotolia; **82** (T) khphoto/Fotolia, (B) NOAA; **83** Photodisc/Thinkstock; **84** (B) Jupiter Images/Thinkstock, (TL) Tim Ridley/©DK Images; **85** John Anderson/ Fotlia/Fotolia; **86** (BL) Elzbieta Sekowska/Fotolia, (TL) Getty Images; **87** (Bkgrd) Dave King/©DK Images; **88** (BL) cbpix/Fotolia, (TL) Hemera Technologies, (Bkgrd) Thinkstock; **89** (TR) Ronald Schmäschke/Fotolia; **90** (Inset) Michael Ransburg/Fotolia; **92** (Bkgrd) Dudarev Mikhail/Fotolia, (B) Eric Isselée/Fotolia, (BL) Frank Greenaway/DK Images, (BR) Getty Images, (C) Jane Burton/DK Images, (T) Rich Lindie/Fotolia; **94** (CR, CL) ©Royalty-Free/Corbis, (TR, TL, C, B) Fotolia, (C) Tom Brakefield/Thinkstock; **95** (L) Comstock/Thinkstock, (T) Goran Bogicevic/Fotolia, (R) Thinkstock; **96** (TC, CL) Getty Images, (BL, BC) Jupiter Images, (TL) W Doering/Fotolia; **97** (Inset) Fotolia, (Bkgrd) Thinkstock; **98** (BR) DK Images, (TL, T, CL, BL) Fotolia; **99** (BR) Acok; **101** (L) ©Royalty-Free/Corbis, (T, Bkgrd) Fotolia, (R) Thomas Northcut/Thinkstock; **102** Fotolia; **103** (TR) Fotolia; **104** (TL, B) Fotolia, (R) Jayjaydy/Fotolia; **105** (R) Martin Wilkinson/Fotolia; **106** (TL, C, Bkgrd, B) Fotolia; **108** (T) Courtesy of Digital Dragonflies, (C) DK Images, (B) Fotolia; **109** ©DK Images; **110** (R, B) DK Images, (TL)

Objectsforall/Fotolia; **111** (R) Bob Langrish/DK Images; **112** (TL) DK Images, (BL) Dreymedv/Fotolia, (TR) Fabrice Beauchehe/Fotolia, (BR) Jan Prchal/Fotolia; **114** (BL) DK Images, (TL) Jupiter Images, (BR, BC) Kim Taylor and Jane Burton/©DK Images; **115** Acok/Fotolia; **116** (TL) Jupiter Images, (R) paulmckinnon/Fotolia, (BL) Thinkstock; **117** DK Images; **118** (T, B) DK Images; **119** (TR, TL, BL, BC) DK Images; **120** (TL, C, BR, BL) DK Images; **121** DK Images; **122** (Inset) Ablestock/Thinkstock, (TL) Cécili'art/Fotolia, (TR) FocalPoint/Fotolia, (TC) SuperStock; **124** (TR, BR, BL) JPS/Fotolia, (Bkgrd) Scott Bufkin/Fotolia, (TL) SuperStock; **125** (T) Getty Images, (CL) Le Chat Machine/Fotolia, (B) Paylessimages/Fotolia; **126** (CL) Acok/Fotolia, (C, BR, BL) DK Images, (TL, CR, C) Fotolia; **127** (TR) ©DK Images; **128** (B) Andrea Moro/Fotolia, (C) NASA, (T) SuperStock; **129** (L) Roman Arcea/Fotolia; **130** (BC, B) Fotolia, (TC) Thinkstock; **131** (TR) Goran Bogicevic/Fotolia, (C) Thinkstock, (TL) Tom Brakefield/Thinkstock; **132** (TR) Steve Byland/Fotolia, (Inset) Thomas Stettler/Fotolia; **134** (Bkgrd) Comstock/Thinkstock; **135** (Inset) David De Lossy/Thinkstock; **136** (B) Daniel Nimmervoll/Fotolia, (T) Getty Images, (C) Natalia D/Fotolia, (Bkgrd) Tazzymoto/Fotolia; **137** (Inset, Bkgrd) Fotolia; **138** (T, BR) Fotolia, (BL) Tyler Boyes/Fotolia; **139** (CL) ©Royalty-Free/Corbis, (BL) Fotolia, (BR) Thinkstock; **141** (TR, Bkgrd) Fotolia, (C) Ryan McVay/Thinkstock; **142** (CC) Fotolia; **143** (TR) ©DK Images; **144** Getty Images; **145** (BL) DK Images, (BR) Mariusz Blach/Fotolia, (T) Stocksnapper/Fotolia, (TR) Thinkstock; **146** (B) ©Royalty-Free/Corbis, (T) Hemera Technologies; **147** (T) DK Images, (B) Jupiter Images, (C) Tyler Boyes/Fotolia; **148** (TL) DK Images; **149** (B) DK Images; **150** (CL) Burtsc/Fotolia, (TL, BR) Getty Images, (CR) Vali/Fotolia; **151** (R, BR) ©Royalty-Free/Corbis, (TL) Domas Orintas/Fotolia; **152** (Inset) ©Royalty-Free/Corbis, (B) Fotolia, (TL) Hemera Technologies; **153** (B) Fotolia, (Inset) Kasi Lodrigue/Fotolia; **154** (B) Fotolia, (T) Sylvain Bouquet/Fotolia, (TR) Thinkstock; **156** (TL) ©Corbis, (R) Brenda Bailey/Fotolia, (BL) Ryan McVay/Thinkstock/PhotoDisc, (BR) Thinkstock; **158** (CL) Avesun/Fotolia, (R) Eppic/Fotolia, (TL) Getty Images; **159** (L) Matthew Antonino/Fotolia; **160** (TR) Manipulateur/Fotolia; **162** (Bkgrd) AVAVA/Fotolia; **164** (CL) ©Royalty-Free/Corbis, (CR, C, B) Fotolia, (TL) Thinkstock, (TC) Tyler Boyes/Fotolia; **165** (B) Shock/Fotolia, (T) Stockbyte/Thinkstock; **166** (Bkgrd) ©Royalty-Free/Corbis, (TR) Getty Images, (L) Human Spaceflight Collection/NASA, (R) Jacques Descloitres, MODIS Rapid Response Team, GSFC/NASA; **167** (T, B) Getty Images; **168** (Bkgrd) ©Royalty-Free/Corbis, (TL) Ben Twist/Fotolia, (BL) Charlie Borland/SuperStock, (R) Tim Ridley/DK Images, (CL) Valeriy Kirsanov/Fotolia; **169** (Inset) Comstock/Thinkstock, (Bkgrd) Fotolia; **170** (T, B) Thinkstock; **171** (BL) Fotolia, (BR) Jupiterimages/Thinkstock, (TR) NASA, (CR) SuperStock; **173** (Bkgrd) Thinkstock; **174** (Bkgrd) Omers/Fotolia; **175** (BR) DK Images; **176** (TL) Lynette Judd/Fotolia, (B) RRF/Fotolia, (TR) Thinkstock; **177** (TR) Jean-Marc Strydom/Fotolia, (B) Thinkstock; **178** (TL) Hemera Technologies, (B) Thinkstock; **180** (TL) Hemera Technologies, (BR) Jupiterimages/Thinkstock; **181** (B) Jupiterimages/Thinkstock, (C) Ron Downey/Fotolia, (T) Scott Patterson/Fotolia; **182** (TL) Hemera Technologies, (B) Outdoorsman/Fotolia; **183** (B) Fotolia, (T) heysues23/Fotolia, (C) Oscar/Fotolia; **184** (BR) Celso Pupo/Fotolia, (TL) Hemera Technologies; **185** (C) Thinkstock, (B) Wollwerth Imagery/Fotolia; **186** (TL) Hemera Technologies, (R) Jupiterimages/Thinkstock; **187** (B) Comstock Images/Getty Images, (C) Getty Images, (T) Mario Beauregard/Fotolia; **188** (TL) DK Images; **189** (Bkgrd) SuperStock, (Inset) Tyler Olson/Fotolia; **190** (TL) fotola70/Fotolia, (Inset) kimberly kilborn/Fotolia, (Bkgrd) Thinkstock; **192** (Bkgrd) George Doyle/Thinkstock, (TL) Hemera Technologies; **193** (Inset) NASA; **196** (Inset) Ivan kmit/Fotolia, (Bkgrd) Thinkstock; **197** (T) Getty Images, (C, B) Hemera Technologies; **198** (BR) Fotolia, (TR) Jupiterimages/Thinkstock, (CL) NASA, (TL) SuperStock, (CR, BL) Thinkstock; **199** (T) Anette Linnea Rasmussen/Fotolia, (B) Creatas Images/Thinkstock; **200** (T) ©MSFC/NASA, (Bkgrd) NASA; **202** (B) DK Images; **203** (B) Paul Moore/Fotolia; **205** (Inset) Colin Keates/DK Images; **207** (BR) Paul Moore/Fotolia, (TR) Stephen Oliver/DK Images; **208** (BR) Bkpardini/Fotolia, (CL) Colin Keates, Courtesy of the Natural History Museum, London/DK Images, (BL) DK Images, (TL) Tim Ridley/DK Images; **209** (TC) DK Images; **210** (C) Chungking/Fotolia, (TL) Hemera Technologies, (R) Natural History Museum/©DK Images; **211** (TR) Natural History Museum/DK Images; **212** (TL, CR, C) DK Images; **213** (TR, BR) DK Images; **214** (CR, B) DK Images; **215** (T) DK Images, (B) Giuliano Fornari/DK Images; **216** (R, Bkgrd) ©DK Images, (T, C, B) Andy Crawford/©DK Images; **218** (T) DK Images; **220** (T) cbenjasuwan/Fotolia, (B)

Colin Keates/Courtesy of the Natural History Museum, London/DK Images, (Bkgrd) MAMZ Images/Fotolia, (R) pgm/Fotolia, (C) Thinkstock; **221** (Inset) Fotolia; **222** (T, CR) DK Images, (CL) Paul Moore/Fotolia, (B) Thinkstock; **223** (T, B) DK Images; **224** (T) ©Andy Crawford/Courtesy of the Senckenberg Nature Museum, Frankfurt /DK Images, (R) Getty Images/Jupiterimages/Thinkstock, (B) Les Cunliffe/Fotolia; **226** (T) Fotolia, (C) Thinkstock; **228** (TR) Colin Keates/Courtesy of the Natural History Museum, London/DK Images; **230** (Bkgrd) Karl Weatherly/Thinkstock, (Inset) Thinkstock; **231** (CR, BR) Thinkstock; **232** (Bkgrd) Getty Images; **233** (Bkgrd) Thinkstock; **237** (TR) Getty Images; **239** (BL) Brand X Pictures, Getty Images; **242** (TL) Hemera Technologies; **248** (CL) ©Steve Gorton and Gary Ombler/DK Images; **250** (TL) Jupiter Images; **252** (C) ©Brand X Pictures/Getty Images; **254** (TL) C Squared Studios/Photodisc/Getty Images, (B) thomas.andri/Fotolia; **255** (B) ©Royalty-Free/Corbis; **256** (Inset) ©Royalty-Free/Corbis; **262** (CL) ©John F. Kennedy Space Center/NASA, (B) Marshall Space Flight Center/NASA, (CR) NASA; **263** (TR) Ames Research Center Image Library/NASA, (TL, CR, CL) NASA; **264** (TL) Ames Research Center Image Library/NASA, (B) Digital Vision/Thinkstock, (CL, BR) NASA; **265** (Inset) Agb/Fotolia, (Bkgrd) George Doyle/Thinkstock; **266** (T) BananaStock/Thinkstock, (BL) Getty Images, (BR) Thinkstock; **267** (BR) atomicrooster/Fotolia, (C) EuToch/Fotolia, (CR) Fotolia, (BL) Thinkstock; **269** (Bkgrd) BananaStock/Thinkstock; **270** BananaStock/Thinkstock; **271** (TR) Hemera Technologies; **272** (R) Getty Images, (B) Thinkstock, (TL) Zedcor Wholly Owned /Thinkstock; **274** (TL) Hemera Technologies; **275** (B) Bec Parsons/Thinkstock, (B) Fotolia, (T) Stockbyte/Thinkstock; **276** (TL) Hemera Technologies; **278** (TL) DK Images; **279** Thinkstock; **280** (TL) Hemera Technologies, (B) Thinkstock; **281** Fotolia; **282** (T) EuToch/Fotolia, (B) Fotolia, (TL) Hemera Technologies; **283** (CL) ©Royalty-Free/Corbis; **284** (L) atomicrooster/Fotolia, (R) Evgeny Deligodin /Fotolia, (TL) Hemera Technologies; **285** Dave King/©DK Images; **286** (TL) Getty Images; **287** (B) Digital Vision/Thinkstock, (T) Getty Images, (B) Giovanni Rinaldi/Fotolia; **288** (C) Steve Gorton and Gary Ombler/©DK Images; **289** (T) Getty Images; **292** (Bkgrd) SuperStock; **294** (CL) EuToch/Fotolia, (TL) Fotolia, (C) Getty Images, (B) Thinkstock; **295** (B) Evgeny Deligodin /Fotolia; **296** (Bkgrd) michelangelus/Fotolia, (T) Nikolai Sorokin/Fotolia, (Inset) Petro Teslenko/Fotolia, (BL) Tradigi/Fotolia; **297** (Inset, Bkgrd) Fotolia; **298** (T) SuperStock, (BL) Thinkstock; **300** ; **301** (Bkgrd) SuperStock; **302** (Bkgrd) SuperStock; **303** (TR) DK Images, (Inset) Fotolia; **304** (L) Fotolia, (T) Getty Images, (R) Thinkstock; **306** (BL) Fotolia, (TL) Hemera Technologies, (R) Stockbyte/Thinkstock; **307** (C) ©DK Images, (R) Hemera Technologies; **308** (B) Fotolia, (TL) Getty Images; **309** (T) Fotolia; **310** (TL) Hemera Technologies, (R) Jack Hollingsworth/Thinkstock; **311** Sly/Fotolia; **312** (TL) Hemera Technologies; **313** (B) ©ThinkStock/SuperStock, (T) Thinkstock; **314** (TL) Hemera Technologies; **316** (CR) Digital Stock, (TL, BR) DK Images, (CL) Marina Krasnovid/Fotolia; **317** (CL) Jupiterimages /Thinkstock, (CR) Wolfgang Kruck/Fotolia; **318** (BR,) ©Gary Ombler/DK Images; **320** (TL) Hemera Technologies; **322** (TR) Digital Vision/Getty Images; **326** (BL) Fotolia, (B) Sroka/Fotolia, (C) Thinkstock; **328** (Inset) ©Jeff Caplan/Langley Research Center/NASA, (Bkgrd) Langley Image Gallery/NASA; **329** (Bkgrd) Fotolia; **330** (B) Ralf Kraft/Fotolia, (T) Thinkstock; **331** (B) Thinkstock; **333** (Inset) Jupiterimages/Thinkstock, (Bkgrd) Thinkstock; **334** (Bkgrd) Thinkstock; **335** (TR) Getty Images, (B) Thinkstock; **336** (BL) Alexander Mirokhin/Fotolia, (CR) DeVIce/Fotolia, (CL) DK Images, (BR) Eray/Fotolia, (TL) Getty Images; **337** (TR, BR) ©Royalty-Free/Corbis, (BL) Getty Images, (TL) Tomas Sobel/Fotolia; **338** (B) DK Images, (TL) Hemera Technologies; **339** (TL) Fotolia, (TR) Thinkstock; **340** (CL) Fomaa/Fotolia, (B) Getty Images; **341** Angelo Giampiccolo/Fotolia; **342** ©Royalty-Free/Corbis, (TL)Creatas/Thinkstock, (C) Fotolia, (CL) Getty Images, (BL) Tootles/Fotolia; **343** (TR) Corbis, (CR) Kirill Zdorov/Fotolia; **344** (TL) DK Images; **346** (TR) DK Images; **348** (Bkgrd) Thinkstock; **350** (TL) DK Images, (TR) Fotolia, (B) Getty Images; **351** (BL)Creatas/Thinkstock, (T) Fotolia, (BR) Getty Images; **352** (Bkgrd) ©Royalty-Free/Corbis, (B) Ecoview/Fotolia; **353** (C) Jupiterimages/Thinkstock; **354** (C) BananaStock/Thinkstock, (C) SuperStock, (B) Thinkstock; **355** (Bkgrd) Steve Mason/Thinkstock; **360** (Bkgrd) Martin Poole/Thinkstock; **361** (Inset) Getty Images, (Bkgrd) NASA; **362** (T, BL) Fotolia; **363** (BR) Fotolia, (BL) NASA; **365** (TR) Getty Images, (Bkgrd) SuperStock; **366** (C) SuperStock; **367** (BR) ©SOHO (ESA & NASA)/NASA; **368** (C)